Mind Mastery For Winning Golf

USING YOUR HEAD TO REACH PAR AND TO ENJOY PLAYING

Robert J. Rotella

Director of Sport Psychology, University of Virginia

Linda K. Bunker

Director of Motor Learning, University of Virginia

A SPECTRUM BOOK

Prentice-Hall, Inc., Englewood Cliffs, New Jersey 07632

Library of Congress Cataloging in Publication Data

Rotella, Robert.
  Mind mastery for winning golf.

  (A Spectrum Book)
  Includes index.
  1. Golf—Psychological aspects. I. Bunker,
Linda. II. Title.
GV979.P75R67   796.352'01'9   81–5876
ISBN 0–13–583328–0   AACR2
ISBN 0–13–583310–8 (pbk.)

Manufacturing buyer: *Cathie Lenard*
Interior design: *Pat Lewis*

10 9 8 7 6 5 4 3 2 1

Printed in the United States of America

This Spectrum Book can be made available to businesses and organizations at a
special discount when ordered in large quantities. For more information, contact:

Prentice-Hall, Inc.
General Book Marketing
Special Sales Division
Englewood Cliffs, New Jersey 07632

Prentice-Hall International, Inc., *London*
Prentice-Hall of Australia Pty, Limited, *Sydney*
Prentice-Hall of Canada, Ltd., *Toronto*
Prentice-Hall of India Private Limited, *New Delhi*
Prentice-Hall of Japan, Inc., *Tokyo*
Prentice-Hall of Southeast Asia Pte. Ltd., *Singapore*
Whitehall Books Limited, Wellington, *New Zealand*

Dedicated to AUNT IRENE, who introduced me to golf and helped me to
realize its challenges and its joys.

BOB

And to PARK, whose love and joy in
life inspired me to believe in myself
and strive to help others find success
and happiness.

LINDA

Contents

Foreword

I have enjoyed playing and promoting the game of golf for many years. In my mind it is one of the greatest activities in which an individual can participate.

During the past years I have seen golfers from every level of playing ability attempt to develop a mastery over this seemingly simple game. I have watched many people ruin their enjoyment of the game by taking themselves and their game so seriously that their playing creates rather than eliminates stress in their lives.

Others work hard on the game, take it seriously, and practice and play regularly. However, they keep their attitude toward the game in perspective. As a result, they learn to play the game quite well while realizing that perfection may never be attained. But they never lose their zest for improvement. People with such an attitude often live long and healthy lives filled with fun and enjoyment on the golf course.

Mind Mastery for Winning Golf is a book that will be extremely beneficial to golfers of all levels of ability. It will help you put your game into perspective and show you how to cope with the pressure experienced while golfing. By controlling your mind, you will not only learn how to golf better than you ever have before, but you will also be able to relax and enjoy playing it more.

This book does not present a quick "fix it" approach to golf, but it will show you how to plan, practice, and play with a systematic approach to improvement and success just as the pros do in the Desert Classic. It will provide you with a personalized guide to attentional control. It will teach you how to manage anxiety and self-defeating thoughts and feelings through the use of relaxation techniques. You will learn how to control your mind when playing with a partner so that such experiences can become more successful and pleasurable.

I highly recommend that people of all ages, from the very old to the very young, read and enjoy this book.

BOB HOPE

Preface

Golfers are becoming more aware of the mental challenges of the game of golf. Recently, we have witnessed a plethora of books that have addressed themselves to this issue. But far too often, authors have only touched the surface of the issues and potential solutions. Usually these books have made interesting reading. Often they have sensitized us to mental hazards and anxieties that we did not even realize existed.

This book takes a different approach. We present an organized and effective approach to the development of the mental aspects of your golf game. The approach is scientifically based and has been effectively used with players of all different levels of skill. If you follow the program presented here, your game will improve. You will come closer to attaining your potential in golf.

Typically, people have treated the physical side of golf as being capable of modification through concentrated practice of proper swing mechanics. Yet, these same people have tended to perceive the mental side of golf as being stable and incapable of change or development through properly prescribed practice. As a result of information discovered by sport psychologists and specialists in motor learning who studied golf, we now know that such preconceived notions are inaccurate. The mental side of the golfer is malleable—it can be developed to enhance your overall golf performance.

Many books dealing with the mental aspects of golf have focused on the problems and mistakes that golfers commonly make. In contrast, this book provides positive strategies which, if followed, will eliminate many of these frustrations, distractions, and the resulting errors so frequently seen in golfers. Self-assessment exercises have been designed to increase your self-awareness of various psychological factors important to attaining your potential in golf. They are an important part of this book. Be sure to use them and learn from them. They are intended to make each chapter more meaningful and valuable to you.

The mental side of golf presented begins with your motivation, takes you through attention and concentration improvement techniques, moves on to the management of your anxieties, and ends by preparing you to understand and improve your golf. As you will find by the time you are through reading this book, individuals are not simply born winners or losers. They are to a great extent the products of their environment, previous patterns of practice, and personal motivation for golf—winners are made.

During your previous golf experiences you may have formed habits, most of which you are no longer aware. Many of these habits may no longer have a logical explanation. Some of these habits may have worked against you and stopped you from performing up to potential.

You do not have to "choke" in stressful situations. You do not have to lack self-confidence. If you will learn to understand yourself, and apply psychological training techniques, you will be able to optimize your ability to play the game of golf and enjoy the process of improvement and growth for the rest of your life.

These goals can best be attained if you follow the road to success discussed in this book. It will not be easy. It probably wouldn't be fun if it were. For most golfers the road to success will require consistent practice of the physical as well as the mental side of golf.

As you will see, good luck will not suffice. Attaining success in golf will come to you much more readily if you plan for success in an effective manner.

Acknowledgments

We wish to acknowledge the influence on our golfing lives of various persons who have stimulated our interests and motivated us to understand the game. In particular, our parents, Billie and F. "Tony" Bunker and Laura and Guido Rotella; and the scholars of golf, DeDe Owens, Jim Flick, Peter Kostis, Davis Love, Jack Lumpkin, Cary Middlecoff, Sam Snead, Gary Wiren, and Ellen Griffin, who have shared their personal love of the game of golf and their quest for optimal performance.

Of particular significance in each of our lives has been the support and encouragement provided by Darlene and Diane. Their positive attitudes as we were writing *Mind Mastery for Winning Golf* made significant contributions to our ultimate goal. Our appreciation is also extended to Frank Dormer, Creative Technologies, Morristown, N.J., who provided the artwork.

1

Are You Motivated for Success in Golf?

Researchers in sport psychology have for years been concerned with the relationship between achievement motivation and sport performance. It is clear that individuals who wish to be successful in the game of golf must understand the importance of their motivational tendencies. Motivational differences frequently separate champions from mediocre or average golfers. With the exception of extremely gifted athletes, success in a sport such as golf requires a moderate to high level of achievement motivation.

Golfers who wish to maximize their potential and markedly improve their golf game, must change their motivational tendencies. Fortunately, one's level of achievement motivation, or the desire to compete against standards of excellence, is capable of being modified. For low-achievement-motivated individuals (hereafter referred to as minimizers), the first step in changing their motivational deficits is self-awareness.

The Golf Attitude and Behavior (GAB) Self-Assessment Inventory is designed to help you determine if you are a *Maximizer* or *Minimizer* (high- or low-achievement-motivated golfer). The GAB is intended to help golfers—so be honest with yourself as you answer each question or your profile will not be accurate and thus of little value. Do not consider the GAB a "test." It is actually a tool to improve your self-awareness and help make low achievers more receptive to a change in their motivational level.

Before reading further, get a pencil, read the instructions, take the Golf Attitude and Behavior Self-Assessment Inventory, and score your profile according to the procedures detailed at the end of the profile. This book will be of greater value to you if you take the test before you consider the remaining ideas.

GAB: GOLF ATTITUDES AND BEHAVIOR SELF-ASSESSMENT INVENTORY

Instructions: This inventory is designed to evaluate your responses to situations relevant to maximizing your potential in golf. The intention of the inventory is to help you become more self-aware of tendencies that might help or hinder your chances of attaining your golfing potential. To get the most out of the inventory, answer each question in a manner that most accurately describes your behavior and attitudes. Do not try and fool the test. You will only be fooling yourself and your chances of benefitting from it.

After reading each question, circle the number under the answer which best describes your behavior.

Strongly Disagree
Mildly Disagree
Mildly Agree
Strongly Agree

	Strongly Agree	*Mildly Agree*	*Mildly Disagree*	*Strongly Disagree*
1. While playing competitive golf, I concentrate totally on my game rather than spend my time and attention socializing with other golfers.	4	3	2	1
2. In a golf tournament I prefer to compete against opponents who play at approximately the same level as I do, rather than against opponents who are not nearly as good as I am.	4	3	2	1

	Strongly Agree	*Mildly Agree*	*Mildly Disagree*	*Strongly Disagree*
3. I spend most of my practice time on my better shots.	1	2	3	4
4. I think more about my future golf performances than about my past performances.	4	3	2	1
5. I work (practice, play, think about, read) year round in order to be successful in golf.	4	3	2	1
6. I prefer to play an average or poor round of golf and win than play well and lose.	1	2	3	4
7. Even though there are weaknesses in my game, I would rather continue scoring as I am at the present time than make changes in my swing which most likely would not dramatically improve my game for at least three months.	1	2	3	4
8. I prefer to read a well-written informative book on golf than to watch a good movie.	4	3	2	1
9. I find that I am constantly comparing my golf game to other golfers' games.	1	2	3	4
10. I worry that I will never improve my golf game.	1	2	3	4
11. I find that my interest and desire in golf changes frequently.	1	2	3	4

GAB: GOLF ATTITUDES AND BEHAVIOR SELF-ASSESSMENT INVENTORY—*Cont.*

	Strongly Agree	Mildly Agree	Mildly Disagree	Strongly Disagree
12. I have trouble hitting tee shots with a driver, but I keep practicing and using my driver rather than regularly switching to a fairway wood or iron.	4	3	2	1
13. I enjoy trying to learn shots which other golfers find difficult.	4	3	2	1
14. I try to play my best even though I know my opponent is better than I am.	4	3	2	1
15. I do not spend much time practicing certain shots such as putting and chipping, because I do not find them very enjoyable or exciting.	1	2	3	4
16. I do not feel that I am as mentally tough as most of the golfers I play against.	1	2	3	4
17. When I lose in a tournament, I take it hard and it bothers me for several days.	1	2	3	4
18. If I have played poorly in a tournament, I spend *most* of my practice time for the next weeks on the shots that I hit poorly during the tournament.	4	3	2	1
19. I find that I spend more time practicing than other golfers.	4	3	2	1
20. I am often self-conscious when people watch me play golf and I find that I don't play as well.	1	2	3	4

GAB: GOLF ATTITUDES AND BEHAVIOR SELF-ASSESSMENT INVENTORY—*Cont.*

	Strongly Agree	Mildly Agree	Mildly Disagree	Strongly Disagree
21. I believe that I have the ability to be a much better golfer than I presently am and that effective practice will pay off.	4	3	2	1
22. I feel that I frequently play poorly because I am unlucky.	1	2	3	4
23. I think that a good golf game is something you are born with rather than something you can develop.	4	3	2	1
24. I sometimes fail to practice so that I have an excuse for not playing well.	1	2	3	4
25. Golf is *too* important to me and sometimes I try too hard to do well.	1	2	3	4

Scoring the GAB: To determine your total score on the GAB and its meaning, simply add up the total of all of the numbers that you have circled.

Maximum Score = 100   My Total Score __78__ 3/2/82

Zone	Score	
A	100–90	Potential Maximizer
B	89–70	Above Average Potential Maximizer
C	69–50	Average Potential Attainment
D	49–35	Below Average Potential Maximizer
E	34–25	Potential Minimizer

Interpreting Your Score The Golf Attitudes and Behavior Self-Assessment Inventory was developed for the purpose of helping golfers increase their self-awareness of personal attitudes and behaviors which may positively or negatively influence the attainment of their maximum potential. The profile has been designed to be useful for males and females of various age groups.

The inventory is not designed to identify winners and losers. The intent has been to help you recognize whether or not your approach to golf has been as effective as possible. The reading that follows will help you to realize that your attitudes and behaviors can be changed in a more effective and efficient direction.

As you will soon realize, your past approach may have been less effective than possible due to bad habits (that may be conscious or unconscious), a lack of knowledge, anxiety, or motivational inadequacies. Try to be honest and open with yourself as you read. Stop occasionally and analyze your past thoughts and behavior. Get to know yourself better. Make a commitment to change. Soon you will be *Mastering your Mind*, lowering your scores and raising your enjoyment.

HIGH VERSUS LOW-ACHIEVEMENT-MOTIVATED GOLFERS

Sport psychologists have identified characteristics related to individuals who are maximizers (high-achievement motivation), and minimizers (low-achievement motivation). *Maximizers* are described as individuals who prefer competitive situations in which they have approximately a fifty-fifty chance of success or failure, set realistic goals, and are more interested in future performance than present or past performance. Maximizers also have a great deal of perseverance, and attempt to finish tasks they undertake. They also tend to remember more of their weaknesses than their strengths following a competitive situation.

Great golfers are constantly going through a process of playing in a tournament, assessing their weaknesses and strengths, then planning practice time to eliminate the weaknesses identified so they can perform better in the future. Their practices are based on past mistakes but designed to remediate them in the future. They do not dwell on feeling lousy or negative about past errors. Rather, they do something about them.

We have all encountered players whose major problem is dwelling on their weaknesses too often. Recognize that it is one thing to work on your weaknesses in practice and something very different to do so during a competitive round. When it is time for competing maximally, you must have confidence in your shots or you will not be ready to perform under pressure. The first way to get ready is through practicing your weaknesses. The second way is through mental training which will be described later.

It should be emphasized that there is absolutely nothing wrong with being a golfer with low-achievement motivation. As a matter of fact, you may even enjoy your game and have more fun as a result of playing with such an approach. However, if you are only playing for fun and have no desire to be a high achiever, do not become frustrated if your score does not improve. Recognize that you cannot lower your score or be a success without effort and self-confidence in your ability.

Minimizers, or low achievers, are described as individuals who prefer extremely easy or extremely difficult tasks, and are more interested in immediate or past performances than in future performance. They are less likely to persevere, less likely to complete tasks they undertake, and tend to remember more of their strengths than their weaknesses following a competitive situation. The golfer who is a minimizer may display a self-concept reflecting a perception of lack of ability combined with a tendency to actively circumvent failure and/or worry about failure. The belief system and action preferences of these individuals tend to be very predictable and consistent over time and across situations, even in the face of contradictory facts.

Often, golfers who fail to improve worry so much about

failure they never get around to doing anything about preventing it from occurring. They may simply avoid their weak skills and focus on their strengths. Golf professionals often speak of students who are unteachable because they won't accept the pro's assessment of their weaknesses. Likewise, many low-achievement-motivated golfers don't think about teaching themselves very effectively.

In order to completely understand the development of the fear of failure which characterizes the minimizer, one more step must be taken. The role of perceived blame or credit (causal attribution) for success or failure in achievement situations must be understood. Causal attributions are the reasons used to explain our own behaviors. The minimizer may prefer to attempt challenges that are extremely easy or difficult in nature. When such a golfer is attracted to an easy situation (a low-goal situation), success is highly likely, and when it occurs, the success will be clearly attributed to the ease of the task. Obviously, the ease or difficulty of a task is a factor external to the individual, so the golfer will not be able to take credit for the success. If difficult or high goals are sought, success is unlikely; yet, even if it is attained, the success will most likely be attributed to external factors such as luck, rather than internal factors such as ability or effort. Often golfers with this type of perception have little confidence in their ability to improve. As a result, little effort is put into careful practice committed to improving.

MINIMIZER—(Low-Achievement-Motivated Golfers)
　　　　　Prefer very easy or difficult challenges
　　　　　Success is attributed to ease of task
　　　　　Failure blamed on luck or difficult tasks
　　　　　Little effort put forth for improvement

MAXIMIZER—(High-Achievement-Motivated Golfers)
　　　　　Prefer fifty-fifty chance situations
　　　　　Success is attributed to hard work
　　　　　Maximal effort expended to improve

In general, minimizers set themselves up for failure. Both their motivation and perception are quite detrimental to further improvement. Recently, while conducting a seminar, Sam Snead reported that other golfers often tell him that he was "lucky to be *born* with a smooth swing." Snead does not perceive his success as due to luck, but rather due to his own hard work. He feels that anyone who wants to improve must hit thousands of practice balls to develop a swing like his. His swing became smooth only through persistent effort and a belief that he would get better and better if he kept with it.

How about you? How often do you blame your lack of success or the success of others to their being born with it? What good does such a perception do your golf game, or your self-concept? Little if any, other than give you an excuse for your own poor performance.

If you wish to start moving in a positive, forward direction, you will need to change your perception. [Emphasize the importance of effort in the success of others, and use the knowledge to help your game.] Likewise, question how great their own innate ability is, relative to yours. Are you sure that all super golfers are more talented than you? Were they born with that talent? Find someone with less natural ability than you. Find another golfer that started golfing late in life. Look for things in others that will increase rather than decrease your motivation. As you watch other golfers, at your local club or on the professional tour, do you really believe they all possess a great deal more physical ability than you? Or have they simply practiced longer and more diligently?

The maximizer (high-achievement-motivated golfer), on the other hand, [sets realistic goals in which there is a fifty-fifty chance of success and failure.] This preference results in the golfer who is high in achievement motivation and who attributes success to internal factors such as ability and effort, and attributes failure to either bad luck or lack of effort. The result is an increase in motivation and effort to improve his or her golf because there still remains full confidence in one's own ability.

It is impossible to find a successful golfer who does not believe in his or her ability. So do not be fooled by the socially desirable statements they may make to others— we all like to appear modest. It is what they say and think to themselves that is important. Watch their dedicated approach to practice. They will completely immerse themselves in becoming a better golfer. Compare yourself to these people. If you find that your behavior is different, don't justify and defend yourself; change for the better.

It becomes increasingly apparent that by their goal-setting preferences, low-achievement-motivated golfers may create situations that minimize their personal responsibility for success and yet blame their failures on lack of ability rather than effort or external factors such as task difficulty or bad luck. The opposite is true for the maximizer, high in achievement motivation, who will simply work harder and set goals in order to be a success at golf.

In summary, the reasons golfers consciously or unconsciously give for success or failure vary between high- and low-achievement-motivated golfers. Minimizers (low-achievement-motivated golfers), tend to blame failure on a lack of ability, while maximizers (high-achievement-motivated golfers), perceive failure as due to a lack of effort. Clearly, the effort one expends is capable of being modified. Physical attributes such as strength, flexibility, tension management, coordination, and timing can and should be modified if you wish to attain your potential. Ability, on the other hand, is quite permanent. If one looks separately at internal causes, lack of ability has a more detrimental effect on self-reinforcement than a lack of momentary effort. Obviously, the low achiever digs a hole that gets deeper and deeper. Even under comparable conditions, golfers with high-achievement motivation credit themselves more for their successes than for their failures, while low achievers credit or blame themselves more for their failures than for their successes.

ARE YOU TRYING TOO HARD?

A high level of achievement motivation may be important to success in golf. However, it is possible to be so highly motivated and so greatly in need of success that you can work against yourself.

[Be cautious of becoming so concerned with your golf success that it controls *you,* rather than you controlling it. Do not allow yourself to become so driven that you are constantly overpracticing and thus becoming overtired and unable to physically or mentally concentrate and practice effectively.]

[Strive for success, but don't become such a perfectionist that you can never think of anything else. Such people will often "burn out" and lose their motivation before they ever attain their goals in golf. A relaxed and well-paced approach to golf is very important. Walter Hagen once suggested to an overzealous partner, "Don't forget to *stop and smell the flowers* along the way."]

Jack Nicklaus suggests that this realistic attitude may merely require that you have fun while you work hard at your golf game. Some have even suggested a sort of positive fatalism so you can recognize that no one hits a perfect shot every time. If you have practiced carefully and given the present situation your "best shot," stop and smell the flowers, even if you fail temporarily.

HAVE YOU FAILED TO IMPROVE
RECENTLY?

Some gifted athletes are quite successful at golf when they first try it. Some actually shoot in the eightys on their first attempt. More and more we are finding that as a result of these early successes, many fine athletes perceive that golf success is a result of their physical ability only. Thus, these individuals may not put the required effort and practice into their game. As a result they don't make much improvement after their early success.

Examine yourself carefully. If you are one of these individuals you must realize how important careful and consistent practices are to successful development of your golf game. Your ability alone will not get you there.

No matter what your motivation has been in the past, you will wish to constantly evaluate your own individual approach to attaining success in golf. Make a commitment now to improve your own performance. It may help to force yourself to admit, out loud, that you are promising to systematically attempt to change your attitude and game. You may even wish to sign a "commitment to improvement" as shown on the following page.

I have decided to find out how good a golfer I can become. I admit that in the past I may not have been aware or self-disciplined enough to come close to maximizing my potential. I am going to read and apply the techniques outlined in this book on a regular basis. I will utilize both mental and physical practice techniques. I will positively deny that I can be much better than assert that I can become a better golfer by faithfully trying these techniques for a twelve-month period.

I will practice mentally every day. I will practice physically as often as I can and when I do, I will practice carefully and systematically. I will stick with my plan, learn to understand myself better, alter ineffective perceptions, and develop new self-control behaviors to improve my ability to perform under pressure.

I make this commitment to myself and I will recruit at least one friend to help me in staying with my plan. I will try and get this friend to make a commitment to the same program. We will check each other once each week.

My Signature: _____ Date: _____

Friend's Signature: _____ Weekly Practice Check:

Yes _____ No _____

2

A Motivational Plan
for High Achievement
in Golf

All golfers desiring success must recognize the importance of believing in their ability and recognizing the important role that effort plays. You cannot deceive yourself into believing that your innate ability will carry you through. The first step to gaining self-confidence is to seek out your weaknesses and practice hard to eliminate them.

How often have you heard Tom Watson, Nancy Lopez-Melton, or your local club champion state that something is wrong with their swing when they are in a slump? Next time, observe what they do about it. You will see that they usually get a lesson and then go to the practice tee and hit hundreds of balls, until they regain confidence in the shot by solving the problem. They do not stop practice until they have their swing back. Most successful golfers follow this same strategy. This approach was learned by them early in life. Persistent practice was the way they developed their golf game originally. It was an important first step in their development of self-confidence in their golf game. The techniques presented later in this book will detail mental training techniques for enhancing your confidence on the golf course, but they all begin with correct self-practice.

This approach also applies to your putting and short game. Recall the recent example of Rex Caldwell discussing his new found confidence in his putting game. It happened as a result of weeks of putting from sunup to sundown, until he believed in his stroke. Again, his putting was improved the same way the rest of his game was learned—

through persistent practice and regular evaluation of his strengths and weaknesses. Clearly, then, if you wish to "master your mind," you must have a systematic goal-setting program designed to maximize your potential.

Hopefully, you are becoming increasingly aware that you, like most, may have areas in which motivation and perception can be strengthened in order to improve upon deficits which may have prevented you from achieving your potential in golf. If you have, make a commitment to the program detailed in this book, and you will be pleased with your improvement!

ESTABLISH REALISTIC GOALS

Step one in the program requires that you develop (in writing) a list of realistic goals for yourself in golf. Both a list of long-range goals and a list of sequential short-range goals need to be carefully identified. (See Chapter 10 for examples of how to set goals for yourself.) This is the most important first step in becoming a high achiever in golf. Do not allow yourself to be lazy in the process. Be sure that each goal is objective and measurable so that your confidence will be able to naturally grow as you achieve each sequential goal on the way to achieving your long-range goal. By objectively detailing your improvement as a result of increased and organized effort, you will see your own real improvement. For example, if you wish to increase your chipping ability, establish a long-range goal of hitting from forty feet away to within three feet of the pin. Appropriate intermediate goals might be to shoot for five out of ten shots to fall a distance within ten feet from the pin, progressing to six feet, and finally three feet from the pin, in a period of two months.

It is important that the golfer realizes that the attainment of these goals may require a great deal of effort. The major value of sequential short-range goals is to allow yourself to personally see your own progress in the development of your golf game. Your goals should set you up for success rather than failure. They should be based on the notion of progressive steps and successive approximations. For instance, do not decide that you wish to hit fifteen greens in regulation and use thirty putts per eighteen holes in six months, if you are presently hitting three greens and using forty-three putts and only wish to practice once a week. Base your goals honestly on your desire to improve and the amount of effort you are willing to put forth. If your goal is to play like the club champion, or a PGA touring pro, be willing to take as many lessons and devote as many hours to practice as they have in developing their games. Look at yourself in comparison to others with whom you wish to compete. Are they ahead of you at the present? Do they have more talent (ability) than you or have they been practicing for years? If the answer to any of the above is yes, then be ready to practice a lot more than you will see them practice. Accept this fact and be happy with it. Don't let it be a frustration to you. If you don't do this, you are being unrealistic, setting yourself up for failure, and in essence thinking like a low-achievement-motivated golfer.

Remember low-achievement-motivated golfers do not realize the value in setting small sequential goals in order to realize long-range ambitions. Long-range goals must be perceived as more important than concern with immediate gratification. Far too often the low-achievement-motivated athlete for the person who is not maximizing his or her potential never plans out how to attain a goal that is months or years in the future. Consequently, low achievers with more talent will be surpassed by high achievers with less talent over extended time periods. Many high achievers actually relish this perceptual weakness in the low achiever, recognizing full well that if it were not so, they would never catch up or surpass them.

BE OBJECTIVE—LIST YOUR
STRENGTHS AND WEAKNESSES

Step two requires you to draw up a master list of all the golfing skills needed for reaching your desired level of proficiency (knowledge of physical skills, strategy, rules, proper equipment, physical conditioning, mental training). The list should be very specific. Each golfer (with the help of a professional and/or golfing friends) must detail, in sequential order, a list of their golf skills starting with their weakest and working on up to their strongest. When this list has been completed, a specific amount of time should be allocated during every practice session for working on one other individual weakness only. As each weakness is alleviated and you reach your short-range goal, less practice time should be spent on it. Time is then increasingly spent on the next weakest skill. This process continues until you have accomplished all of the short-range goals which will lead up to your long-range goals. At this point you should reevaluate your golf game, search for your weaknesses again, and set new goals. (See Chapter 9 and Appendix for detailed approach to setting up this program.)

The low-achievement-motivated golfer tends to spend more time practicing strengths than weaknesses—especially when surrounded by friends or other golfers. Admit it to yourself—it is a great deal more fun to do what you do well in practice. Practicing your strengths most likely makes you feel good; practicing your weaknesses typically causes you to feel somewhat anxious or even depressed. As a result many golfers avoid these unpleasant feelings by not working on their weaknesses. It is much better to feel anxious in practice for a while and master the skill (hitting out of bad lies, hitting a long iron, uneven lies, etc.), than to avoid the unpleasantness in practice and have it occur during an important match.

The best way to improve yourself in any endeavor is

to constantly seek out your weaknesses and do whatever is necessary to remediate them. In assessing your weaknesses, it would be wise to determine which skills are most important to golfing success. For instance, you might take into account the facts that a statistical look at the game of golf by *Golf Digest Magazine* has shown that golf is 43 percent putting, 25 percent wood play, 13 percent chipping, 7 percent short irons, 4 percent medium irons, 3 percent long irons, and 5 percent trouble shots. The relative contribution of these areas should all be considered when deciding which weaknesses are the most detrimental to your own golf game.

How about you as a golfer? Have you been avoiding practice on your putting and chipping? Do you tend to find these skills boring and unenjoyable? If so, you need to realize that a change of attitude is required if you are to become a more successful golfer. If you aren't willing to change, don't expect to be golfing up to your potential.

For the next week, record your golf performance utilizing the chart on the next page. This process is designed to allow you to systematically record your performance during an actual round of play. When you utilize this tool, be sure to fill in the actual yardage and par per hole for the course on which you are playing. This form is designed to help you evaluate the immediate outcome of your shots, *Physical Aspects,* and the *Mental Aspects* which may have influenced your ability to stroke the ball.

It may be helpful to begin by focusing on the external (or physical) results of your shots. For each hole, record under the shot or club selections, the result of each stroke (above the diagonal line):

$\sqrt{}$ = on target
R = right of target
L = left of target
O = beyond target (over hit)
U = short of target (under hit)

This record of the effect of your shots will help you identify which skills are being effectively or ineffectively executed. Unfortunately, the analysis may reflect the result of the shot, but not the underlying cause.

You should now begin to evaluate the mental or internal aspects of your round of golf. You should focus on the psychological thoughts which are going on in your head as you play. For each shot, record the appropriate description for the internal (mental) aspects of your game:

NT = *N*egative *T*hinking, or negative self-confidence
LA = *L*ack of *A*ttention control
BT = excess *B*ody *T*ension
FR = *F*ailure to use a *R*outine
OA = *O*ver *A*roused, or tried to hard on the shot
UA = *U*nder *A*roused, or went to sleep on the shot
CMC = *C*omplete *M*ental *C*ontrol

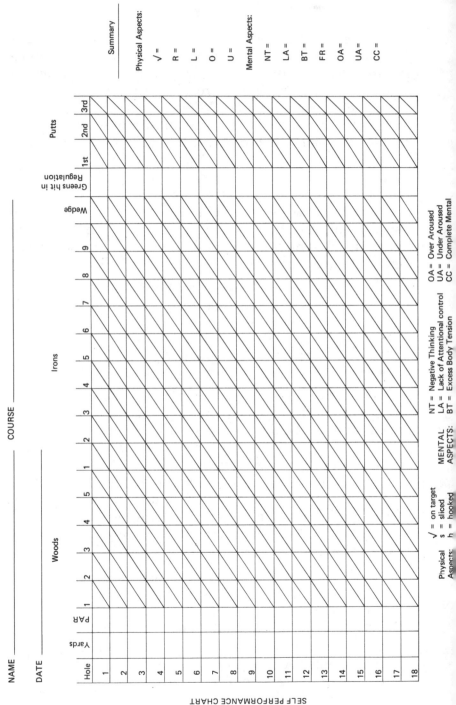

NAME _____ **COURSE** _____

DATE _____

Hole	Yards	PAR	Woods 1	2	3	4	5	Irons 1	2	3	4	5	6	7	8	9	Wedge	Greens hit in Regulation	Putts 1st	2nd	3rd
1																					
2																					
3																					
4																					
5																					
6																					
7																					
8																					
9																					
10																					
11																					
12																					
13																					
14																					
15																					
16																					
17																					
18																					

Physical Aspects: √ = on target   s = sliced   h = hooked

MENTAL ASPECTS:
NT = Negative Thinking
LA = Lack of Attentional control
BT = Excess Body Tension
OA = Over Aroused
UA = Under Aroused
CC = Complete Mental

Summary

Physical Aspects:
√ =
R =
L =
O =
U =

Mental Aspects:
NT =
LA =
BT =
FR =
OA =
UA =
CC =

SELF PERFORMANCE CHART

When you are comfortable with both the physical and mental scoring techniques for this observation form, attempt to combine these two sets of notations so that you will begin to see the relationship between the mental and physical aspects. The following observations made by Tom about his round of golf may illustrate the types of information provided by a completed form.

Let us look at Tom's play on the first hole. He teed off with his driver and went to the right of his target ("R"). He noted that he was quite tense and so recorded a "BT" as his mental state. On his second shot he hit a 9-iron and overshot his target to the right (R and O) while berating himself for his last shot (negative thinking). His third shot was a pitching wedge which he hit beyond his target, but was in complete mental control (O/CMC). His first putt was slightly rushed, and underhit (U/FR) while the second putt was on target!

At the end of Tom's round of golf, he sat down and quietly analyzed his game. His summary table was very helpful to him in pointing out that he had several tendencies which he could practice to overcome. Tom has a slight alignment problem which causes him to hit to the right of his desired target and to underestimate his target distance. On the mental side, Tom is a rather negative thinker who will benefit greatly from learning to "master his mind."

Compare your on-the-course strengths and weaknesses to the amount of time devoted to each area in practice. Successful golfers spend proportionately more time on their weaknesses and on their short game. Do you? Of course this does not mean that you should overlook your strengths. Be sure to practice them enough to keep them as strengths. Don't think so much about your weaknesses that you lose your confidence and become discouraged.

When you are practicing your weaknesses, don't let yourself get disgusted or frustrated. If you do, chances are you will become less motivated. Do what the pros do. Imagine your practice paying off, and helping you play well in a tournament or some other important match. Help set

NAME _Tim_ COURSE _Westward_

DATE _April 8_

SELF PERFORMANCE CHART

Hole	Yards	PAR	Woods 1	Woods 2	Woods 3	Woods 4	Woods 5	Irons 1	Irons 2	Irons 3	Irons 4	Irons 5	Irons 6	Irons 7	Irons 8	Irons 9	Wedge	Greens hit in Regulation	Putts 1st	Putts 2nd	Putts 3rd
1	375	4	R BT											b NT			O FR		u FR	✓ CC	
2	172	3	✓ CC															ø	✓ CC	✓ CC	
3	391	4			L OA							✓ CC	✓ CC					ø	u UA	✓ CC	
4	351	4	L NT		RO NT										✓ FR			ø	O NT	✓ CC	
5	419	4	L NT			R ØT								✓ CC			✓ CC		u NT	✓ BT	✓ BT
6	154	3											✓ CC	✓ CC			✓ CC		LA NT	✓ CC	
7	513	5	R OA		R UA									✓ NT	✓ CC			ø	✓ CC	O NT	✓ BT
8	387	4	R NT		R FR	R ØT									✓ CC		✓ CC	ø	O NT	✓ NT	✓ BT
9	340	4														✓ CC			✓ CC	✓ NT	✓ CC
10	216	3	LV NT														u UA	ø	✓ BT	✓ NT	
11	418	4				✓ CC	✓ CC											ø	u CC	✓ LA	✓ BT
12	315	4	R NT		RO NT									✓ CC	✓ CC			ø	u UA	LA LA	
13	360	4	✓ BT												✓ CC		u UA		R NT	✓ CC	
14	449	4	R NT												✓ CC	✓ CC		ø	R CC	✓ CC	
15	340	4	L OA				L FR		R NT						✓ CC	✓ CC			✓ CC	✓ CC	
16	537	5																ø	R NT	✓ CC	
17	154	3										✓ CC						ø	✓ CC	✓ CC	
18	391	4	✓ CC																R UA	✓ LA	LA

Physical Aspects: ✓ = on target, s = sliced, h = hooked

MENTAL ASPECTS: NT = Negative Thinking, LA = Lack of Attentional control, BT = Excess Body Tension, OA = Over Aroused, UA = Under Aroused, CC = Complete Mental

Summary

Physical Aspects:
✓ = 36
R = 16
L = 7
O = 7
U = 12

Mental Aspects:
NT = 19
LA = 2
BT = 7
FR = 5
OA = 3
UA = 6
CC = 31

yourself up for success and increased motivation by mastering the art of self-encouragement.

In the future, if you play poorly or lose a match, instead of losing confidence in your ability, look for your weaknesses and then do something to improve them. For example, if your Self-Performance Chart points out a weakness in utilizing long irons and hitting the sand wedge, develop a practice strategy to remediate this problem. As you improve these weaknesses in your game, you will realize that you do have talent and that the right attitude and sufficient effort in practice does make a difference. The result will most likely be that you will have the confidence to achieve your goals in golf. You will be on your way to becoming a high-achievement-motivated golfer.

Remember, think about both your strengths and weaknesses after competition, whether you win or lose, by actively seeking them out. While playing, think positively about your strengths and be confident. You are on your way to changing yesterday's weaknesses into tomorrow's strengths.

BUILDING CONFIDENCE IN YOUR GOLF GAME—PROGRAMMING YOURSELF FOR SUCCESS

It is virtually impossible to find a champion golfer who lacks self-confidence. Some may be very vocal in stating their confidence. Others may keep it to themselves or even express to others that they aren't good so as not to offend anyone or be considered a braggart. But in every case, champions are filled with self-confidence.

Very often the only difference between the champion and many others is belief in one's own ability. One of the most common problems encountered by sport psychologists are individuals who have the ability to perform the desired skills or tasks but do not believe in themselves.

How many times have you heard it said that a certain golfer "plays like a winner" and that another "plays like a loser," or that if certain golfers ever realize how good they are, they would be champions. Golf is indeed a mental game.

It is amazing how little effort in the past has been dedicated to the development of the mind of a winner when so much effort has been directed at developing the swing and strategy. In recent years techniques have been developed by sport psychologists for just this purpose and have proven to be effective. Before detailing such techniques for you to use, let us explain their rationale so you will increase your awareness and understanding and therefore be more likely to utilize them regularly.

Your golf self-concept is your personal concept of the kind of golfer you are. This concept was primarily developed as a result of your previous golfing experiences. Included are all of your successes and failures, moments of pride as well as shame, feedback or comments made by friends, parents, coaches, instructors, opponents, or yourself. Unfortunately, with the exception of a few fortunate individuals, the majority of golf experiences may have been labeled as failures due to the emphasis in our society on shooting a good score or being a success early in life. If, from early in your introduction to golf, your experiences could have been all successful there would be no problem with self-confidence. We must, however, function in the world as it is and therefore we must learn to function effectively with the given situation.

Recognize and accept the fact that your self-concept will not change overnight. But you can change it if you will make a commitment to the techniques described in this book. The techniques have worked for many others, and they will work for you if you desire to discover your potential and are willing to practice the physical and mental aspects of your golf game in order to attain it. The decision is yours.

3
Planning for Success the Way the Pros Do

Most golfers have at one time or another experienced a momentary loss of confidence. Many other golfers can identify with a rather permanent lack of self-confidence in their golf game. For most of these golfers, their swing and game may be very effective on the practice tee or when competing against someone that is weaker. But place these golfers in situations where they are not so self-confident and their game may rapidly deteriorate.

The negative effects of a lack of self-confidence do not stop with game play. Individuals limited in self-confidence are likely to be lacking in persistence toward becoming a successful golfer. As mentioned earlier, why practice hard on the physical and mental aspects of golf if you do not believe that by doing so you can become successful? Golfers without self-confidence are also the individuals most likely to quit or lose their motivation when faced with failure. It has been consistently demonstrated that the more self-confident an individual is, the more active their efforts to achieve success will be.

The aspiring golfer must understand the extent to which perceived ability will influence actual performance. Hanns Linderman, who crossed the Atlantic in a canvas raft all alone in seventy-two days stated: "Once we contemplate success, it is already in the making. For that reason, I sank my resolve so deeply in my mind that I had virtually no choice but to succeed."[1]

[1] From Schultz, J. and Luthe, W. *Autogenic Training*. New York: Grune and Stratton, 1959.

The confident golfer expects to hit a good tee shot, hit the approach close to the pin and sink the putt. Such a golfer does not doubt that the shot will go where aimed. Years of research support the concept of the power of this expectancy. Studies related to the effects of drugs and nutrition on sport performance, utilizing placebos, have documented the fact that the *expectancy* of performance being improved as a result of an artificial aid is far more influential on performance than the actual value of the aid. In other words, athletes given placebos or meaningless drugs, who expected to improve performance, did in fact improve. Similarly, if they expected performance to decline, it did—even when no outside influence was imposed.

The golfer on a "streak" is quite clearly self-confident and needs no help. But the problem with so many golfers is that self-confidence varies drastically from moment to moment. Hit one or two bad shots and suddenly you are expecting to mis-hit the next shot, and probably will. A few more shots and you have lost your confidence and are headed into a slump. You may become distracted, start thinking about the mechanics of the swing instead of target, or you may even change an efficient swing to one much less efficient. Now you really have problems and have reason to be losing confidence.

If you wish to become a consistently effective and confident golfer you must prepare in advance. Your preparation should include tying in your goal-setting program with your self-confidence-training program on a regular basis. Before detailing this daily approach, let's explain the most effective ways of building self-confidence in your golf game.

BECOMING SELF-CONFIDENT

The first step in a confidence-building program is to take personal responsibility and accept the fact that *you can train yourself to become self-confident*. Self-confidence is reflective of both (1) being able to perform the desired skill, and (2) believing that you have the ability to perform effectively in a variety of situations. Clearly, both physical and mental training are required. If you are a golfer who is sure that you are physically capable of executing, but are failing to do so because of a lack of confidence in that ability in the competitive environment, then you should direct your thoughts mainly to the mental training aspects of your game. If you are not sure that self-confident expectations are your problem, ask yourself the following questions for insight.

Recall your expectations immediately prior to recent rounds of golf or competitive matches. Did you doubt that you would play well? Did you question your ability? Did you worry that your opponent was out of your league? Did you worry about embarrassing yourself? Do you sometimes question your ability to ever attain your goals? Do you tend to dream of losing or making mistakes on the day or days preceding your rounds?

If your answer to any of these questions is *yes,* you should regularly practice the following strategies. These techniques have been developed by sport psychologists to facilitate positive thinking.

MENTAL REHEARSAL: WINNERS SEE WHAT THEY WANT TO HAPPEN; LOSERS SEE WHAT THEY FEAR MIGHT HAPPEN

It is well known that golfers use mental rehearsal both on and off the golf course. Jack Nicklaus, Tom Watson, Nancy Lopez-Melton, Carole Mann, as well as the duffer, may all use some form of mental imagery. *The difference is in the picture.* Confident golfers have clear pictures of themselves executing the shot perfectly. The golfer lacking in confidence imagines an ineffective result and because of the related anxiety fails to produce as clear a picture. Furthermore, many golfers lacking in confidence fail to be able to control their mental picture. When many of these golfers practice mentally, they hit the ball out of bounds rather than straight, or swing quickly rather than smoothly. It appears that these problems are anxiety related. If you find these problems occurring when you mentally rehearse, you should practice inducing relaxation prior to your mental practice (outlined in Chapter 6). With relaxation and regular practice, you will soon develop control over your mental rehearsal and be on the way to developing the mind of a self-confident winner.

CONTROLLING THE BODY WITH THE MIND

If you wish to be a consistent and efficient golfer, you must realize that your body will do what you instruct it to do. But you must learn how to communicate with your body.

The programming of success in sports through the use

of the imagination has been gaining in popularity and utility, particularly since its introduction by Dr. Maxwell Maltz in his book *Psycho-Cybernetics*. Many professional golfers as well as highly motivated athletes in other sports have benefited from the use of related techniques.

Our body learns and reacts similarly to both actual and imagined experiences. If you have ever walked down a dark, deserted street in a strange town and suddenly been startled by a noise, or awakened in the night from a bad dream, you are well aware that your body reacts emotionally and physiologically as if both were real experiences. You are scared. Likewise if you sit on your back porch and close your eyes and imagine sinking a twenty-foot curler, your body responds by relaxing. Your muscles learn from this kind of practice because they are stimulated by messages sent by the brain. The difference between this mental rehearsal and physical practice is that the stimulation is just below the threshold level required for muscle movement in the imagined situation.

Years of research and application have consistently detailed the important role of combining visualization with physical practice to build self-confidence in one's ability to perform successfully. Sam Snead has often spoken of replaying his round in his head while showing and correcting all of his errors. He recalls that his last thoughts before going to sleep at night after a round are to always play the course perfectly—a most effective technique for preparing himself for confidence in the future as well as getting into a relaxed and confident frame of mind.

The moment that an experience or a belief about yourself enters your mind and forms a picture, it becomes subjectively true. It does not matter whether or not it is. Your performance on the golf course will be influenced by the way you picture yourself. Picture yourself standing up on the first tee and hitting OB (out of bounds). Chances are you will lose confidence. Imagine missing a three-foot putt on eighteen and you'll tighten up and most likely miss it!

Picture a successful shot before hitting it and you will have made a major step in the right direction. You will have begun to program yourself for success.

SELF-EFFICACY TRAINING—THE POWER OF POSITIVE THINKING

Henry Longhurst noted recently:[2]

> I suspect that the best form of practice for the rank-and-file golfer is, if he gets the chance, to settle down and watch some of the best professionals before a tournament and let them do the work. I think especially of the Masters at Augusta, where they provide bleachers for the spectators' comfort behind the players in the two practice areas. Here the student of the golf swing can sit and assimilate all the finer points, hoping that some may seep through into his own uncertain efforts.
>
> One thing I have always thought important, and that is to choose as a model a player of stature approaching your own. A short stocky individual, for instance, would not have so much to pick up from George Archer, who is six foot, five inches, as from, say, Gene Sarazen, who in his seventy's still made golf look so supremely simple.

Longhurst clearly understood the value of visual imagery to mastery of the golf swing. But instead of suggesting it, he instead argued that you should simply watch someone similar to yourself who swings smoothly. Visual imagery is even better than watching someone else swing because you do not have to fool yourself into thinking that you are Gene Sarazen because you may see *yourself* swinging perfectly in your imagination.

[2] Longhurst, H. "Is practice really productive." *Golf Digest*. April, 1978 (p. 30).

EXTERNAL IMAGERY

Your mental practice should include a variety of techniques on a regular basis. The first sort is known as external imagery and should be completely a visually imagined experience of yourself executing various shots perfectly. Imagine playing each shot perfectly—just the way you planned it. As it relates to the mastery of specific golf skills it is best to imagine shots that you are currently practicing physically. If you are playing in a tournament, picture yourself playing the course you will have to play. Picture any bad situation you might get into and imagine successfully overcoming it (for example, OB on one and still shooting a great round). See yourself successfully hitting a long iron out of the rough. We suggest that you end this sort of mental practice at least two days before the start of the tournament. Use only positive pictures on these days. Fill yourself with confident thoughts.

INTERNAL IMAGERY

The second type of mental rehearsal that you should practice on a regular basis is known as internal imagery. It involves a proprioceptive or "feeling" type of mental rehearsal and is usually nonvisual. This is the type of "feel" practice so frequently mentioned by Bob Toski. Feel your grip—lightness in your fingers, thinness in the club; feel your backswing begin—feel your arms begin to move but not your hands. Feel the slight tension across your back at the top of your backswing.

You should analyze your swing and mentally practice developing this feel so that you will be able to reproduce both a visual and a proprioceptive feel prior to each shot when you are on the course. Both are crucial to becoming a successful golfer. Both internal and external rehearsal can be learned if you practice them regularly and combine them with physical practice. There is no short cut. Planning for success will take effort but it will help insure that your efforts will attain the desired result.

Your visual rehearsal should also include rehearsal of your strategy. If you decide that you are going to attack the course, picture yourself attacking it successfully. If you decide to be cautious, visualize yourself playing safe. How long will you stay with your strategy? Picture yourself sticking with or changing it, given a different situation. The key is to be prepared. Don't get anxious or in trouble and quickly make an emotional decision to change your strategy that will only hurt your play. You may also wish to imagine your preround routine, get to the practice tee early, stretch, decide how many balls to hit, imagine practicing chipping, pitching, and putting, reporting to the first tee. Imagine hitting a great tee shot with all your friends and opponents watching. Imagine feeling great and playing great.

Mental rehearsal can be practiced at almost any time of the day: the time spent waiting for a client or your family, the time spent at the barber shop or beauty parlor, half-time of the football game, or intermission in a TV show. Do not let your thoughts wander aimlessly—use those moments for some positive thinking about yourself and your golf game. It will improve your game as well as relax you.

Your mental rehearsal may be centered around positive images of the skills you are trying to improve. Review your last golf lesson, or the last time you hit a great drive. Visualize yourself doing the movements and mentally experience the feeling of accomplishment. Picture the rhythmic *tempo* of the swing—the easy takeaway, the graceful swing through the ball to a balanced finish. Then when you actually play, you should be able to step up to the ball with confidence since you have executed a good swing many times before in your mind.

The important role of confidence in getting prepared on the day before an important round is well described by the great golfer, Macdonald Smith:[3] "It seems to me, that you should practice only with those clubs you were playing well with—to work the good *stuff* into your system, so to speak, instead of trying to work the bad stuff out." This same approach should be applied to your mental practice on the pretournament day. It is important at this final moment to practice those skills which you are the closest to mastering, in order that your confidence remains high.

The time to practice those shots and clubs that you have trouble with is after the tournament or between matches. But do not forget—eventually they must be mastered on the practice tee if you wish to be truly confident during play.

After the tournament, continue your practice, review the shots that gave you trouble. Imagine yourself executing those shots smoothly and effectively each time. For example, plan your chip shots carefully. Don't just try to get the ball close to the hole but see yourself sinking the shot. Play one of your more difficult home-course holes in your mind. Carefully analyze the tee shot and hit a good drive. Visualize your approach shots and execute them well. Check the line of your putt, imagine taking the putter straight back and through with a relaxed, rhythmic stroke. Observe the ball rolling to the hole and disappearing.

These techniques have been found to be the most effective and durable for improved golf. Many others have been tried, but tend to be quite momentary. Strategies such as (1) closely observing the swing of another successful golfer with whom you can identify, (2) making self-confident monologues prior to performance, or (3) trying new equipment (new putter, wedge, etc.) will all be helpful to an athlete's confidence on certain occasions but their effects are only temporary. The strategies related to the mental side of golf emphasized in this book *work* and will have a greater probability of having a permanent effect. You will be surprised

[3] Longhurst, H. "Is practice really productive." *Golf Digest,* April, 1978 (p. 30).

when you actually get on the course how much confidence you have built up, and how much better your game is!

TECHNIQUES FOR DEVELOPING
INTERNAL IMAGERY

Lie down, close your eyes, and imagine the following:

1. Feel comfortable and balanced, stepping up to the ball.
2. Feel the weight of your body being slightly forward on the balls of your feet. Feel more weight on your rear foot than on your target-side foot, (Your target-side foot is your left foot if you are a right-handed golfer.)
3. Feel a slight tension on the inside of your rear leg as it moves inward in the direction of the target.
4. Feel the target-side of your body stretch in preparation for the backswing. Feel the arms begin the backswing with the lower body turning and following. Feel a slight tension in the back of the target-side shoulder. Feel the target-side arm and side remain extended. Feel the relaxed sensations in your rear arm and side.
5. Feel your lower body initiate the downswing and slide toward the target. Feel the arms and hands follow the lower body with a smooth gradual increase in acceleration as your legs and target-side arm pull the clubhead down. Feel the lower body twist just ahead of the hands leading the clubhead through the ball, toward the target.
6. Feel yourself swing smoothly through the ball. Feel yourself finishing underneath and behind the ball.
7. Remember the feelings of this perfect shot.

4
Control of Attention

The game of golf makes great demands on one's ability to control the width and direction of attention. Clearly, attention changes constantly while playing a round of golf. If you wish to be a consistent and effective golfer you must understand these attentional demands and learn how to control them.

WIDTH AND DIRECTION OF ATTENTION

Width of attention can be described on a continuum from a very narrow focus on one small thought or object (such as making contact with the ball), to a broad focus on many thoughts or objects (such as evaluating the weather, wind, lie of the ball and club selection). We are all aware that our minds frequently drift along this continuum but are we able to control it as we desire? Do we even know where our attention should be along this dimension at differing times and situations on the golf course?

Direction of attention can also be conceptualized as varying along a continuum—from focusing on the self (inner thoughts and feelings) to externally focused (the golf course, and other people's thoughts).

ATTENTION

Width of Attention:
   BROAD = a wide variety of elements
   NARROW = one object or thought

Direction of Attention:
   SELF = inner thoughts and feelings
   EXTERNAL = outside influences and decisions based on
the environment

ATTENTIONAL FACTORS IN GOLF

Let us look for a moment at attentional factors as they relate
to a typical golf shot. Imagine that you are 150 yards away
from a small green with a large trap at the front, water
on the left, a slight breeze in your face. It's the eighteenth
hole and you need a par to make the cut for the champion-
ship division of the club tournament. In this particular situation you initially need a broad external focus to gather all

of the important information. Next, you must switch to a broad, self-focus to examine abilities and tendencies pertinent to how you are striking the ball on this particular day. Once these decisions are made, and the club and type of shot to be played are selected, you must now switch to a narrow–external (target) focus of attention. The information has been put into the "computer" and you must now visually focus on one external thought: perfect execution of the desired shot. Next, you need to narrow your focus on yourself and feel the perfect shot you have just imagined. Your last thought should once again be narrow and external (target projection). At this point you need to simply swing and let the swing be an automatic response to the swing which your mind has just programmed.

After execution of the shot, maintain the narrow–external focus and observe the results. Shift to a narrow, self-focus and capture the feeling of the shot. Finally, with a broad–external focus analyze the shot for correct and incorrect decisions and store it in the memory for future decisions. Then, at some later date the information will be available through the use of a broad, self-attentional focus.

Far too many golfers get locked into a narrow, self-focus (thinking body mechanics) during the swing. This attentional focus is appropriate during the learning or early practice phase, but it is most inappropriate during a round of golf. Your attentional focus must be appropriate to your objective. If you are working on some specific skill during a practice round, your attention might be more narrow than during a match.

Be sure you understand this important difference between attention in practice and performance. Prepare by changing attention in practice to a more narrow, external focus during the last days prior to competition. It is time to start getting your mind off mechanics, and let the skill run off automatically.

The information gained from your body and its self-directed attentional focus is beneficial in learning "feel," but is detrimental during the actual swing. You must be able to focus externally if you wish to be able to visualize a successful shot. Constantly attempt to become aware of your strengths and weaknesses in this area. Strive to improve your weaknesses and maximize your strengths so that ultimately you will be able to shift your attentional focus as required.

The following sequence may appear to be long and complex, but will follow a logical pattern as you implement it.

SEQUENCE OF ATTENTION FOR A GOOD GOLF SHOT[a]

A. *Preliminary Aspects*
   1. Broad external focus—gather the information needed to assess the requirements of the shot
   2. Broad self-focus—examine your personal abilities and preferences
   3. Narrow external focus—select club
B. *Set-Up Phase*
   4. Narrow external focus—concentrate on the target
   5. Narrow self-focus—feel the perfect shot
   6. Narrow external focus—think through the intermediate target (one to two feet ahead) to aid in alignment to final goal
C. *In-Swing Phase*—Shot runs off automatically—think target
   7. Narrow external focus—observe the results
   8. Narrow self-focus—capture the feeling of that shot
   9. Broad external focus—analyze the shot relative to previous correct or incorrect decisions
   10. Narrow self-focus—visualize and feel the correct swing

[a] You must practice this sequence until it is automatic.

RECOGNIZE YOUR ATTENTIONAL STYLE

Do you tend to "fly off the handle," "lose your cool," and get emotionally upset while playing golf? If you do, you probably have a tendency to be external in your attentional style. Chances are that you frequently make impulsive decisions regarding shot selection. You will often make irrational and inappropriate decisions. Seldom will you stick to a game plan which has been carefully thought out.

You may not presently be able to "feel" and "read" your body. You may react emotionally to bad breaks and fail to realize that bad breaks will even out so you might as well forget about them. You would be much better off to try and remember the good breaks rather than dwell on the bad ones.

Some golfers get so wrapped up in their feelings and emotions that they fail to respond to the environmental factors pertinent to a particular golf course or the weather. On the other hand, the self-focused golfer can be cool and collected which is obviously beneficial much of the time. But often such individuals become too involved with internal and self-related thoughts. These individuals have problems in changing strategy when required. They tend to remain tied into a set strategy even when it needs to be modified. Often such individuals are great students of the game and will make great teachers, but think too much while performing. "Paralysis by analysis" can prevent a golfer from being able to play up to his or her ability.

How about the golfer with too broad an attentional style? This type of individual will have a tendency to have too many thoughts on his/her mind, with the result being an inability to consistently stick with one game plan or swing. Practice is often flighty and changing with little consistency. Such golfers may shift from being an aggressive golfer to a very conservative golfer for no apparent reason. The golfer with a broad attentional tendency may be over-analytical and often will overreact to bad breaks or great play by the opposition. Instead of recognizing that on a certain day putts may not drop due to rough greens or a small pebble, such golfers will completely alter their putting stroke. This type of golfer may lose in match play despite the best round of his life and decide to completely rebuild the golf swing.

ATTENTION–DISTRACTION SELF-EVALUATION INVENTORY

Instructions: Circle the response which best describes your response to the situation described next to it.

Situations	Strongly Agree	Mildly Agree	Mildly Disagree	Strongly Disagree
1. If I make a mistake on a shot I have difficulty not thinking about it while hitting my next shot.	4	3	2	1
2. When teeing off on a tight fairway I think about going out of bounds.	4	3	2	1
3. I prepare to hit shots without carefully comparing my capabilities to the demands of the shot I'm about to try.	4	3	2	1
4. I wonder what others think about how I play.	4	3	2	1
5. I am self-conscious about my lack of distance off the tee and I think about it when I'm hitting.	4	3	2	1
6. I am distracted by worries of missing short putts on important holes.	4	3	2	1
7. When I golf with others I get so involved with socializing and talking with them that I don't concentrate very well on my own game.	4	3	2	1
8. It is difficult for me to think of only my target as I hit a shot.	4	3	2	1
9. I find myself thinking ahead to how I must do on the remaining holes in order to shoot the score I want.	4	3	2	1

Situations	Strongly Agree	Mildly Agree	Mildly Disagree	Strongly Disagree
10. During a tournament I find myself overanalyzing my mistakes rather than thinking of hitting the shot I am about to hit perfectly.	4	3	2	1
11. I find that when I am playing golf I think of other unrelated things.	4	3	2	1
12. If I am about to hit a shot and someone behind me moves or talks, it distracts me and causes me to hit my shot poorly.	4	3	2	1
13. I fail to concentrate and use a preshot routine when I practice hitting golf shots.	4	3	2	1
14. I find it difficult to visualize vividly the shot I am planning to hit.	4	3	2	1
15. I am so involved with understanding my golf swing that I analyze it constantly while playing.	4	3	2	1

Scoring the Attention-Distraction Inventory: Add the point value for each of the responses selected, and compare your score to the following scale:

Maximum Score = 60   My Total Score _____

Zone	Score	Attentional Control Level
A	60–54	Considerably Below Average
B	53–43	Below Average
C	42–30	Average
D	29–22	Above Average
E	21–15	Considerably Above Average

Golfers with a narrow focus have a tendency to spend most of their time on a few skills which may not be that crucial to success. For example, we all know individuals who practice all woods and long irons, with no work on short irons or putting. Golfers with this style do not analyze the full range of skills and strategies and therefore practice inefficiently. Such golfers may play great on certain days or on particular courses but will be limited in their success due to their narrow attentional style.

Try to be open and honest with yourself. What are your tendencies? Where might you change? Gather information from your friends, teachers, or golf partners. How would they describe your attentional style? Do they agree or disagree with your evaluations? How is your attentional style affected by competition? The next chapter will discuss how anxiety may affect your attentional style and its implications for learning to control the width and direction of attention.

PROBLEMS OF THE HIGHLY MOTIVATED GOLFER

The high-achievement-motivated golfer's interest in improvement can also serve as a disadvantage during competition. High achievers may realize on match or tournament day that they may not have mastered all aspects of their golf game enough to be a winner in the competition. This frequently brings forth a question from high achievers concerning their focus of attention. Such individuals understand that in practice a self-directed attentional focus will help them utilize proprioceptive information to eliminate or at least improve on a detected flaw in their swing. The high achiever realizes that to reach his or her playing potential, each flaw needs to be eliminated. But the high-achieving golfer also understands that by focusing on improvement and centering attention internally on performance, the golfer's opportunity to win this competition will not be maximized. The question is, "Do I stop being concerned with improvement and focus externally to maximize performance; or do I concern myself with the future and continue to think, analyze, and learn throughout the tournament?"

Unfortunately, there is no easy answer to this dilemma because of a variety of related factors. A golfer who wishes to continue learning and practicing, and who has a self-focus and "plays through" a tournament, must realize that this choice may cause him or her to make some errors. A golfer who continues to analyze strokes during a tournament will be performing at a conscious rather than an unconscious or automatic level. In other words, understand what you are doing. You are preparing for the future, not the present. Accept this decision and don't let yourself become disappointed with performance errors.

Certainly if you can't wait any longer and it is time for you to compete, you must temporarily forget further improvement. Concentrate externally on the target during the swing and let it happen at an automatic level. In other words, go play your best and be happy with it. Remember, getting discouraged and thinking negatively seldom does anything helpful for your game.

LEARNING TO CONTROL ATTENTION
AND IMPROVE CONCENTRATION

Why is it that a basketball player can stand at the free-throw line with 10,000 people screaming and throwing objects in the air to distract attention and calmly go through a pre-shot routine, focus on the target, and quite consistently make the desired shot while most golfers, even touring pros, fall flat on their face when a car honks its horn or backfires 300 yards away?

All golfers have particular strengths and weaknesses in their attentional control. Anyone wishing to master the game of golf with its complex attentional demands must practice techniques designed to improve these abilities. Much like the physical side of golf you need to improve your attentional weakness and continue to maximize your strengths. For most golfers, efforts should be spent in two main areas: (1) control the direction and width of attention and develop the ability to switch from one particular style to another (for example, narrow–self to broad–external focus), and (2) improve the length of time that you can maintain your concentration (attending to the immediate present rather than past or future thoughts). Both of these attentional factors are greatly hindered by anxiety, and thus achievement-oriented golfers must prepare themselves if they wish to perform effectively in stressful situations.

CONCENTRATION IMPROVEMENT TECHNIQUES

The following techniques should be practiced in a quiet room.

Step 1. Hold a picture of one of your favorite golf holes in front of you. Study the picture. Study the hole. If any distracting thoughts cross your mind, block them out. Repeat the word "TARGET" and get your mind back on the golf hole shown in your picture. See how long you can focus your attention on the picture. Time it the first few times you try it.

Practice recognizing distracting thoughts as soon as they enter your mind and eliminate them by repeating the word "TARGET." Remember, it is seldom that anyone will play a round of golf without being distracted. You must not stay distracted for an extended period of time.

Each week record your longest concentration time for the week and chart your improvement while in a relaxed environment.

Step 2. When you can maintain your concentration in Step 1 for five minutes without being distracted, begin to practice in a distraction-filled environment (other people, TV or radio on, cars driving by, etc.). Again test your ability to concentrate at the start by timing yourself. When you can maintain concentration for five minutes in this environment, move to Step 3.

Step 3. Practice maintaining your concentration while having some friends, family, or golfing partners attempt to distract you. Have them make personal statements about your physical appearance, your golf swing, your ability to perform under stress or anything which might make you feel self-conscious. Learn to deal with such statements at an intellectual rather than an emotional level. If you let them affect you emotionally, they can destroy your golf game. When you can concentrate without being distracted in this situation for approximately three minutes, begin to practice controlling the width and direction of your attention.

TECHNIQUES FOR CONTROLLING WIDTH AND DIRECTION OF ATTENTION

Establish a routine to be used every time you hit a golf ball (practice or match) such as the one which follows:

Suggested Routine

Relax and take deep breaths as you walk.

Look at the fairway lie, assess the weather conditions and potential hazards.

Look at the target. Decide on the shot required.

Evaluate the distance and select the required club.

Stand behind the ball holding the club in front of you. Picture your target and the shot you want to hit, including identifying an intermediate target about one to three feet away, and the flight and roll of the ball.

Step up to the ball, place the rear foot and again sight through the intermediate target to the target.

Address the ball, setting the target foot, and then readjust the rear foot.

Feel the shot with your whole body. (If it does not feel good—STOP—and start over again. Do not get lazy or self-conscious, and go ahead and hit it. Most likely if you do it will not result in a good shot.)

Feel the shot. Waggle if you prefer.

Again picture the desired shot and while feeling the shot, think target.

Think target and swing.

WAGGLE FOR FEEL

In addition to the internal imagery, you may want to make use of a waggle prior to every shot. (The waggle is a pre-swing routine which is helpful in getting the hands and arms moving as well as inducing relaxation.) Ben Hogan has suggested that one of the main functions of the waggle is to teach you the "feel" of the upcoming shot. The rhythm of the waggle should reflect the rhythm of the anticipated shot. It should be performed at the same rate and rhythm of the actual shot. Obviously, the waggle has an important function and is an individual preference which, if chosen, should be practiced seriously.

Next, picture the target and identify an intermediate target about one or two feet away from the ball and in line with the target (narrow–external focus). Think target and swing to the target (narrow–external focus). Watch your shot, remember the feeling (narrow–self focus), and analyze the effectiveness of your last shot (broad–external focus). Take a deep, slow breath and walk to your next shot.

Practicing a routine such as the one previously described, or a similar routine, will not only get you into the good habit of changing the width and direction of your attentional focus, it will also prepare you for control in stress-ful conditions because you will be familiar with it and may be able to effectively control your attention.

Eventually you will want to try these techniques on the practice tee while competing with friends. Remember, build for success.

5
Anxiety and Performance

Anxiety can have a detrimental effect on the body as well as on the mind. It refers to that state of mind when you start to worry about possible negative results that might occur. Psychologically, anxiety may develop when you become fearful of losing, making a mistake, going out of bounds, or missing a three-foot putt. If you diminish the ability to control your attention your performance may deteriorate. On the other hand, if you can learn to control your anxiety and focus your attention purposefully, your golf game is likely to improve.

In order to maximize your ability to control your anxiety, it is important to assess your present state. The following Self-Assessment Test is designed to help you gauge your own anxiety.

SELF-ASSESSMENT TEST FOR GAUGING ANXIETY IN GOLF

Instructions: Circle the response which most agrees with your response to the situation described next to it.

Situation	Strongly Agree	Agree	Disagree	Strongly Disagree
1. On important shots my hands feel cold and I lose my feel.	4	3	2	1
2. On important shots I rush my swing even though I am not comfortable over the ball.	4	3	2	1

SELF-ASSESSMENT TEST FOR GAUGING ANXIETY IN GOLF—*Cont.*

Situation	Strongly Agree	Agree	Disagree	Strongly Disagree
3. During tournaments I try "new" shots which I have never consistently practiced.	4	3	2	1
4. When I stub my club in the grass on my backswing, I continue and hit the ball anyway.	4	3	2	1
5. If I mess up on the first few holes, I tend to mess up the rest of my round.	4	3	2	1
6. If I have to hit a short pitch shot over a sand trap to a tight pin, I imagine my shot landing in the trap.	4	3	2	1
7. When I am standing over a three-foot putt to win a match, I worry that I might miss.	4	3	2	1
8. I am very critical of myself.	4	3	2	1
9. When the wind is blowing in my face, I grip my club tighter than normal.	4	3	2	1
10. There are certain clubs in my bag that I would rather never hit.	4	3	2	1

Scoring: Add each of the responses selected.

Maximum Score = 40   My Total Score = _____
                          (add total responses)

Zone	Score	Tension Level
A	40–36	Considerably Above Average
B	35–29	Above Average
C	28–21	Average
D	20–14	Below Average
E	13–10	Considerably Below Average

Scoring. If you determine from your self-assessment test that you have more anxiety than most others, do not be alarmed. That is what the rest of this chapter is all about. It will help you to realize that it is alright to be anxious and perhaps it is actually appropriate and useful. You must learn to read anxiety and use anxious thoughts and feelings to your advantage, rather than allowing them to overwhelm you and destroy your game.

The self-assessment was designed to help you realize that the more anxiety you have, the more important it is that you control it. With the ability to control your anxiety, no matter how much you may initially experience, you can definitely become a better golfer.

THE FIGHT OR FLIGHT SYNDROME

It does not matter whether your reasons for becoming anxious are real (I can't hit a straight tee shot) or imagined (I don't think I can hit a straight tee shot). The body will still go into a state of preparedness for danger known as "the fight or flight" syndrome. Have you ever awakened in the middle of the night from a bad dream in a cold sweat? Have you ever had a close call in your car and reacted by sweating and breathing quickly? It does not matter that there was no real danger. Just the thought of danger can initiate the "fight or flight" response with real bodily reactions. The "fight or flight" syndrome is an automatic response mechanism designed to help us in dangerous situations. It is a marked hindrance to us when we are attempting to concentrate and execute a golf shot.

When you become anxious about a golf shot, even if for no apparent reason, a signal is sent to the hypothalamus which releases a hormone that triggers the nearby pituitary gland. The pituitary sends a hormone (ACTH) which tells the adrenal glands to release several other hormones, some of which you are familiar with—adrenaline, norepineph-

rine, and cortisone. These hormones are designed to prepare your mind and body for an emergency situation. Your
heartbeat and breathing speed up and panting allows you
to eliminate carbon dioxide quickly. The muscles of your
body in general begin to tighten. You no longer accurately
differentiate between muscles that should be relaxed rather
than tensed. Even the muscles surrounding your lungs and
bronchial tubes tend to tighten, which results in shortness
and shallowness of breath. To make up for this shortness
of breath, breathing becomes more rapid.

   If the situation were severe enough, you would actually

"choke" to death. Such is often the case with individuals who have supposedly drowned but have no water in their lungs. The anxious thoughts you perceive while playing golf may indeed cause you to experience the choking sensation to a degree. Your heartbeat may speed up, with rapid breathing and increased sweating. You may feel tired due to excess tension and carbon dioxide. You may experience a loss of control of your attention and a tendency to make "dumb" decisions. Have you ever needed one more shot to shoot a personal best, or beat a golfer you have never before defeated, and found yourself trying a shot you have never before attempted, let alone executed? Have you ever completely changed your playing style, or hit before you had made up your mind, because your mind was moving too quickly and was confused?

At this time you may be aware that your digestive system shuts down, the esophagus contracts and the gastric juices stop flowing. This can make you feel nauseated and is a good reason why you shouldn't show up on the first tee on tournament day with a full stomach! In order to maximize the efficient use of your larger muscle groups, blood vessels near the surface of the skin, as well as in the hands and feet, close down and divert their blood supply to the larger, deeper muscles. Thus, you can understand the sensation of cold hands or feet when you're nervous and why a "touch" or "fine feel" sport like golf is so greatly affected by anxiety.

WHEN PSYCHING UP HELPS

Many golfers, especially the great ones like Nancy Lopez-Melton or Jack Nicklaus, have used this syndrome to their advantage. They have called on that flow of adrenaline at a crucial time to hit the ball that little bit farther. For them, *when they are playing well* and *are confident,* it works and is helpful. But even for them, when they don't understand the situation and they try a little harder, when they are in a slump and have lost their confidence, the extra adrenaline can cause them to hook out of bounds. Thus, an important distinction must be made. It is one thing for a self-confident, successful golfer who has been slightly bored and underaroused to try and "psych up" at crucial times to maximize performance. It is quite another situation for a golfer lacking in self-confidence, or even the same golfer when not playing well and low on self-confidence, to attempt to "psych up" rather than "psych down" and lower what is already heightened anxiety and arousal level.

It is well documented that there is an inverted-U relationship between arousal level and performance. In other words, for each golfer, there is a moderate level of arousal at which golf performance will peak (see Fig. 1). If you are above or below this level your performance will deterio-

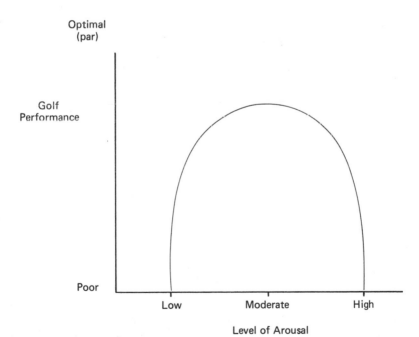

Figure 1. A moderate level of arousal will produce maximum performance. Arousal levels which are too high may produce poor performance (that is, you clutch), while too low a level of arousal produces similar negative effects ("not up for the match").

rate. Most golfers have a problem being overaroused and thus most of the techniques in this book are designed to control overarousal and anxiety-related problems. Of course, if you are bored with a course or your opponent, or just plain golfed out, your problem is underarousal; relaxing more would certainly not be beneficial to your game. It is at times like these that it may indeed be a good idea to start talking to yourself, even negatively, to induce a little anxiety and get yourself up to your peak level. But be sure that you understand yourself and your situation before you do.

Your self-confidence may vary greatly from day to day, hole to hole, and opponent to opponent. It is quite possible to be fully confident and relaxed against one opponent and completely lacking in confidence and uptight against a different opponent, or even the same opponent on another day. This is why, of course, you have been told so often to play the course, not the golfer. But the issue is far more complex—you must understand yourself and how anxiety and arousal will affect your performance before you can learn to self-regulate it to maximize your performance.

CYBERNETICS

One of the most well documented facts that is available to us today is the understanding that the body is controlled by the mind. If we wish to master or control the golf swing, we must know how to tell the body to swing.

Bob Toski is capable of placing a ball on the back edge of a two-by-four and hitting it cleanly with a new three-wood, as if it were sitting up on the grass. Many golfers have a swing developed well enough to allow them to perform this skill. Why then are most of them unable to even start their downswing when confronted with this "trick" shot? They are anxious. Their perception of their ability

is quite different. Their mind will not even allow their body to try it. Prior to hitting, Toski visualizes a successful shot and can feel himself effectively executing the shot. Most golfers cannot even swing under such pressure, because their mind will not allow them to execute the shot. Their thoughts are anxiety filled and they can only imagine themselves shattering their hands as well as their clubhead by hitting the two-by-four. Others may allow themselves to swing but induce so much anxiety in the process that they lose the coordination that usually typifies their swing. The result: they smash their hands and clubhead—the exact picture they had in their mind.

In fact, any golfer with the ability to swing a club effectively can execute this two-by-four skill. The golf swing should be an automatic swing, which can be carried out with little conscious effort.

The science of "cybernetics" has great potential for explaining to each and every golfer how to maximize their potential. Far too many of our current practices tend to limit our potential. However, cybernetics as a concept can provide an explanation for the comparative study of the human brain and nervous system with complex electronic computer-programmed machines. Cybernetic study has taught us that our brain and nervous system make up a complex goal-striving mechanism. Depending on how we operate this automatic guidance system, it can work *for* us as a success mechanism or *against* us as a failure mechanism. If you wish to plan for success you must present the brain with positive or success-oriented goals. These goals, of course, need to be realistic and you must be willing to practice and progress a little bit at a time. If you present the brain and nervous system with negative or failure-oriented goals, it will probably function as a failure mechanism.

Your automatic guidance system operates in the same fashion as a computer. Compare your golf swing to a guided missile. Both have a goal—the hitting of a target; both (if correctly programmed) have been programmed to succeed; both have the machinery to achieve the goal. Heat and pressure sensors are all connected to a mass of electrical wiring for the computer, while you, the golfer, have your senses of sight, touch, and hearing, and your brain and nervous system made up of billions of nerve cells, each with its own wiring of axons, dendrites, and synapses; both use feedback data carried through the system by electrical impulses, and both can use and store data in memory banks. Feedback allows the system to perform in a smooth and coordinated manner.

Every time you experience something, you either create new neural pathways (patterns in the gray matter of your brain) or strengthen the patterns which already exist. These patterns are stored (like magnetic tapes in computers) and can be replayed whenever a past experience is recalled. Your job is to learn how to replay the successful experiences rather than the negative ones, therefore strengthening them to such a degree that they become an automatic activity. Programming for this automatic response is what planning for success in golf is all about.

Although both pieces of machinery are extremely complex, the human "computer" is vastly superior. It can not only store vast amounts of information and carry out programs, but it can also program itself. Other machines can not. Humans are even able to respond to subtle changes in emotional and physical states.

We are able to self-correct and intellectualize. Unfortunately, we do not always utilize our equipment very effectively. Many golfers simply respond emotionally to their experiences. If we play well, we respond with pride. Emotionally we feel good. We are confident. We practice more and program ourselves in very self-enhancing ways. On the other hand, if our game is going poorly, we may also respond emotionally. We may feel embarrassed and ashamed. Emotionally we may feel lousy and lose confidence. We may start practicing less and begin to program ourselves in very self-defeating ways. Our game gets progressively worse. Soon we are in a slump and become disgusted with our golf game.

But we do not have to simply "respond" to our experience of success or failure in an emotional fashion. We can learn how to intellectualize these experiences and control our emotional responses to certain situations that are likely to occur. Even the pros hit balls out of bounds or into the water! Even pros stay buried in sand traps and miss two-foot putts! Why then should you let such mistakes ruin your entire round? Why should you let your emotions cause you to make more mistakes than you need to?

One way to control your response to situations is through the use of your imagination. Scientists have emphasized that the human brain and nervous system cannot differentiate between a real and an imagined experience. Research in sport psychology and motor learning has consistently demonstrated the superiority of combining mental practice with physical practice in both the learning and mastery of athletic skills.

The best way to successfully help acquire the desired neural pathways is through the use of mental rehearsal and positive visual imagery. Mental rehearsal is particularly useful in the learning phase. These techniques can be used any time that you are learning a new shot or making a change in your swing. When practicing mental rehearsal you should study the picture of your swing and thoroughly analyze it part by part, over and over again. It is just as important however, that you feel your swing—try to cue in on the proprioceptive feedback that you get. Continually analyze and correct until you have the picture and feel that it is right.

As you learn the swing and can consistently repeat it smoothly in practice, visually imagine yourself, as vividly as possible, swinging perfectly. Be sure to imagine a wide variety of situations. Remember, at this point you are preparing yourself to be relaxed and confident in the competitive situation. The more visual practice you do, the more experience you will have in your mind of having been there before, performing successfully, and the more confident you will be. Visual imagery should be used on a regular basis for any shot about which you are not completely confident; hitting a ball out of a divot, out of deep rough, buried in sand, on a steep side hill, up or downhill lie, hitting the perfect tee shot on the first hole, making a three-footer on eighteen. If you really want to be good, be willing to spend the little time required to plan for confidence when competing in possible anxiety-producing situations.

ANXIETY AND YOUR SELF-TALK

Why Are You So Mean to Yourself?

You realize by now that your thoughts influence your emotions which in turn control and direct your behavior. It should, therefore, be easy for you to see why the things you say to yourself are also going to greatly influence how well you play golf.

At the present time you know how to control your imagery to build confidence and help control your anxiety.

Now let's see how to control your self-talk to further build your confidence and manage your anxieties.

Because you initiate, continue, and end the way in which you talk to yourself (your self-talk), it is under your control. Far too often, however, you set yourself up for failure instead of success. You become confused when you are anxious and forget that you are supposed to help, not destroy, yourself. It may be particularly helpful at this point to try to re-assess your own anxiety levels through the test shown on page 54–55.

Are You Overly Critical of Yourself?

Why should you be your own worst enemy? Why always put yourself down? Why not start talking to yourself in a way that will help your performance?

Think about it carefully. Would you pay money to go to a golf instructor who continuously put you down, told you that you were a klutz, swore at you, criticized you, and constantly told you that you were a loser and a choke? Probably you wouldn't. Why then do you destroy your performance by saying these things to yourself?

For most people the reason for personal negativism is due to a tendency to always want to compare oneself to others. If the standards that you compare yourself to are unrealistically high (such as a golf pro, or someone who spends much more time or money than you on golf), chances are you will treat yourself like a failure and may constantly criticize yourself.

WINNERS AND LOSERS TALK DIFFERENTLY TO THEMSELVES

In order to help you to better understand the role of positive self-talk, let's compare the difference between the way successful golfers speak to themselves versus the way unsuccessful golfers talk to themselves. The unsuccessful prevent themselves from consistently becoming relaxed and confident on the golf course.

Successful golfers begin talking to themselves when they are getting ready to go to the course. For example, listen to the self-talk of a successful golfer: "I feel good. I can't wait to get out on the course. I've been really hitting the ball. Hey, there's a nice breeze blowing. I love to play on a windy day. It gives me a big advantage over the others. I wonder how much I can talk them into betting."

Once their round begins, successful golfers are able to completely immerse themselves in their golf. When they get into trouble on the course they evaluate their options carefully. For example: "O.K., I'm behind this tree. There is a slight opening. I could try to go through it. Maybe I should play safe and go for a bogie. No, I think I'll go for it. I can make that shot. I like this shot."

Such golfers clearly expect to make the shot and all thoughts are focused on this occurrence only. No doubts or second thoughts. "Good, I hit it real sweet. Just missed the green. I made a good decision. I'm in pretty good shape."

Following a successful round such a golfer might say, "Great round. It sure was fun. I can't wait to play again tomorrow. I wonder if anyone wants to play nine more today. No! Oh, well, I think I'll come to the club early tomorrow and hit some mid-irons. I wasn't hitting them quite perfectly today."

Certainly the self-statements of successful golfers cause them to become emotionally excited, pleased, and confident about their golfing. This emotional reaction will greatly influence their future performance.

On the other hand, individuals lacking in confidence, who are anxious about their golfing, actually encourage failure by the way they talk to themselves. For example, listen to the anxious self-talk of a golfer on the way to the golf course, "I sure hope I'm not hooking too badly today. That darn first hole, if only I can get by it without going out of bounds. I get behind on that first hole and I press the rest of the way. I hope I don't have to hit any three irons. I haven't hit one in weeks."

Out on the course, this golfer may continue this negative self-talk. "How did I ever let myself get into this rough. No way I'm going to get out of this. I might as well swing away. There's no sense playing safe scoring as poorly as I am. On second thought, maybe I should. Oh, what the heck, go ahead and hit it." During the swing this golfer may still be questioning, but hits it anyway—right out of bounds. "What a dummy. No way I should have hit that shot. I should have played a different shot."

After finishing the round such golfers often say, "I can't wait until I get out of here. This game is so ridiculous. It drives me crazy. I'm such a loser. I choke every time. Well, maybe if I don't touch my clubs for a couple of days I'll be better off."

Most clearly this type of self-talk causes golfers to become emotionally depressed and prone to quitting and losing confidence in their golf game.

Just as negative self-talk can be detrimental to your mastery of golf, positive self-talk can help it. You can help yourself a lot by simply listening to your self-talk. Recognize when you are setting yourself up for failure and discouragement. Whenever you find yourself making anxiety-provoking self-statements or thoughts, tell yourself: (1) Take a deep, slow breath, (2) STOP, (3) help yourself, (4) make a positive self-statement, (5) consider what is the most rational and realistic way to deal with this situation, (6) make your decision and stick with it—no doubts allowed.

You will soon realize that when you are self-confident and relaxed as a result of using these techniques, your attention will naturally focus appropriately. You will no longer be locked into your inner thoughts and fears. You will no longer have to be a victim of your emotions. You will no longer have to feel negatively about your emotions, but will be able to use them to positively direct your practice and understand your cognitions. The nature of your *self-defeating* statements can be altered to become self-enhancing. Examine the following self-defeating and self-enhanc-

ing statements and notice how your perspective can be
easily changed.

ASSESSMENT OF YOUR SELF-STATEMENTS

Thoughts that are self-enhancing or self-defeating for the attainment
of your potential.

Self-Defeating	*Self-Enhancing*
1. There is no sense in practicing and trying to improve. I have no talent and could never be any good anyway.	1. I have seen many effective golfers who seem to have very average physical abilities. With my attitude and desire, I can get better if I practice correctly.
2. I'd like to improve my golf game but I don't have time. My work and family require too much of my time.	2. I'd like to improve my golf game. I need to schedule my time more effectively. Maybe I can go in to work an hour earlier and take my working friends, spouse, or children golfing with me occasionally.
3. I'm too old to start trying to improve my golf game. People will laugh and think I am foolish to put so much time and effort into a game like golf.	3. Golf should be a great game for someone my age. People will really admire me if I get better and improve my game. I will get a chance to interact with people of all ages, and make new friends. It will help keep me feeling young.
4. The only way to get good at golf is to have a lot of money so you can have great lessons. This has been true for anyone who is good at golf. I wish I were born rich and lucky.	4. To get good at golf I will need quality lessons. On my budget I will have to set aside some money each week or give up something I don't really need so that I can get them. I must find a solution.
5. I don't think I will try hard to improve my golf game. If I try and fail to get better, I will look bad and people will think I must really be lacking in talent.	5. I will try hard to improve my golf game. I'm sure I can get better. But no matter what happens I will find out what my potential is. I will know that I gave it my best shot. I will never have to regret that I didn't at least try.

Self-Defeating	*Self-Enhancing*
6. There's no sense in practicing and trying to improve. You're either born a good golfer or you'll never get good. Look at Sam Snead. The lucky man was born with a perfect swing.	6. I am going to practice effectively on a regular basis. Sam Snead and other great golfers say they couldn't swing very well, hit the ball far, or score well when they started. But they hit thousands and thousands of shots and got better. I'll be persistent, try the same, and see how good I can get.
7. There is no sense in trying to develop my golf game. It doesn't look like much fun and there is no exercise at all involved.	7. Golf sure looks like a fun game that I will be able to play for the rest of my life. It offers a great physical and mental challenge. It can also provide beneficial exercise if I will walk when I play.

After reading the self-defeating and self-enhancing statements, take a moment and think of your own typical self-statements. Do you set yourself up for success or for failure? From now on after you complete a practice round of competitive golf, try to recall your thoughts and self-statements prior to, during, and following your round. Search for tendencies. Do you tend to help or hurt yourself? Now do the same thing for practicing your favorite shots and the shots you least enjoy practicing. Do you talk yourself out of practicing your poorer shots? How does this lead you to hit these shots poorly in tournaments and then dislike them more which again causes you to dislike practicing them? Be honest and get to know yourself. Confront your ineffective tendencies. *Do not expect problems and/or weaknesses to get up and disappear.* Face them, and work consistently to maximize your potential.

Golf is a tough game. It is not easily mastered. Situations constantly occur in matches when the golfer who strives for success must learn to manage stress. A strategy known as "coping" can be most helpful in learning to manage these stressful situations.

A coping strategy requires that you try to imagine, or, if possible, recall all of the different stressful situations with which you have ever dealt. How did you respond to the situation? What did you say to yourself at the time? What were you thinking? Did you manage the situation effectively? How could you handle the situation better? What should you have said to yourself that would have been better? Try to think of a great golfer that you admire. How would they have dealt with it? How are you going to react to this situation if it occurs again?

Think through each of these questions carefully. They are of *utmost* importance. Before your next round of golf try to imagine all of the stressful situations that could occur and plan how you will talk to yourself and cope with the situation. Be prepared for anything. Soon you will be ready to handle any situation.

Recognize that, in the past, most of your self-corrective feedback may have been directed at physical skills. You must now start learning how you are likely to respond emotionally and mentally to specific situations. For example, how do you respond to missing a two-foot putt? What happens to your attention? Does it affect you emotionally on your next shot? Are you mentally distracted? How does it influence your mind on your next short putt?

If you wish to golf up to your potential, you must learn to control mentally distracting emotional responses. Maybe you don't even know if you are distracted. One way to find out is to compare your thoughts, images, and self-statements when you are relaxed, confident, and playing well, with your thoughts, images, and self-statements when you are playing poorly, or playing under stress. The goal will be to consistently think the way that you do when you are confident and relaxed. If you aren't, don't hit your next shot. You are not ready to play!

Learn to "Read" Your Anxieties. Many golfers believe something is wrong with them if they are anxious prior to an important round of golf. This is not true. Even the greatest pros in the world have fears, worries, and anxieties. They too worry about missing short putts, going out of bounds on the first hole, blowing a lead on the finishing holes, leaving themselves in sand, or embarrassing themselves in front of others. In this regard, they are no different than the average golfer. The contrast is in the way they respond to these anxieties.

Effective golfers read their anxieties and effectively cope and manage them. Ineffective golfers either fail to read their anxieties, or read them but fail to manage them. Less successful golfers typically remain lost in the "work of worry."

The effective golfer looks ahead, anticipates the skills needed to play well, and practices weeks in advance of a tournament. At this point the golfer appraises whether or not he or she is anxious about any of these skills, and asks: "Can I hit a shot from a downhill lie?" "Can I hit a variety of sand shots?" "Can I control my swing while hitting into the wind?" "If I need a four-foot putt on the last hole, will I be confident of making it?"

If you are anxious about any of these questions, just admit it and then start practicing in order to prepare for the competition. In a similar fashion, you should anticipate mental responses to situations that have previously elicited anxious thoughts. Possible distracting thoughts should be recognized, especially if they have interfered with performance. As a result, effective statements and thoughts should be prepared for use when confronted with stress.

For example, an effective golfer anticipates anxiety over short putts and practices these skills; but also admits that stress may cause distractions on short putts, especially after one has been missed. Such a golfer makes sure that he or she responds to these distracting thoughts by employing appropriate and effective relaxation techniques. Attention is then focused on the appropriate direction prior to stroking the putt.

The ineffective golfer, on the other hand, responds quite differently to the same anxiety. Frequently the result is to go ahead and putt while distracted, and therefore be unsure of the line or how to stroke the putt.

Tournament players usually preview the golf course prior to playing. Perceptually, the ineffective golfer may mentally block out the difficult parts of the course. In essence, they do not even see the tough holes, perhaps hoping they will disappear when it is time to play. Unfortunately, they will not go away, and in fact, they will become even more significant as competitive stress increases. The golfer who avoids these difficulties will not be prepared to play as well as possible.

Other ineffective golfers see the difficult parts of the course, but may respond mainly by worrying. They worry that they will miss the putt. They worry about going out of bounds, hooking, slicing, etc. While worrying, they go ahead and hit the ball, usually poorly. Clearly, you cannot be concentrating on what you need to do, if you are distracted by worries about what you might do wrong. Worrying is a waste of energy if it is not used to mobilize your energy into positive action!

Positive Thinking. Positive thinking is part of your key to "golfing out of your mind." You must believe in yourself. You must believe that you can improve. At tournament time, you must think positively. Your last thoughts prior to hitting a shot must be positive.

But positive thinking alone is not enough. You must read your anxieties and work to eliminate them if you wish to think positively and be confident. It will not just happen. You cannot fool yourself into being confident. This is why

reading your anxieties and learning to cope with stress is so crucial to your future golfing success. You must effectively use your mind and body to develop confidence.

Let us consider for a moment that you have a tournament to play tomorrow. How should you best prepare yourself for this event? Let's begin when you are ready to retire for the evening prior to the match. Get in bed, close your eyes, and go through the relaxation training exercises. Picture the course that you will be playing tomorrow, and imagine yourself playing each hole perfectly. Hit every shot as you would ideally like to hit them. Hit every tee shot, sink every putt. Feel good about your swing. Feel confident. You have read your anxieties and prepared. You have reason to believe in yourself. Relax and drift off to sleep. If you wake up or at any time have anxious thoughts cross your mind, tell yourself to "STOP," relax, and induce positive self-statements and positive imagery. Feel and see yourself swinging perfectly. And drift off to sleep with these positive images and thoughts.

A GOLFER'S MIND AND BODY IN ACTION

An analysis of your attitudes toward unexpected events may help you assess your own ability to cope. The following are descriptions of golfers who maximize or minimize their potential through their coping and self-talk strategies.

Two Different Responses to Tournament Stress

Golf Related Situation: (Potential Source of Stress)	Golfing Potential Minimizer: (Copes with Stress Ineffectively)	Golfing Potential Maximizer: (Copes with Stress Effectively)
1. 1:30 A.M. Golfer lies in bed unable to go to sleep the night before golf tournament.	Golfer lies in bed worrying about tomorrow's tournament. Thinking about weaknesses in golf game and difficulty of the golf course. Worries of failure dominate the mind. The golfer stays awake long into the night.	Golfer recognizes that worrying and staying awake will hurt performance in tomorrow's tournament. So golfer *stops* negative thoughts, redirects thoughts to positive images of tomorrow's play and goes through relaxation exercise. The golfer falls asleep and gets a good night's rest.
2. 7:30 A.M. Golfer accidentally oversleeps wake-up time by an hour.	Golfer jumps out of bed mad at person responsible for wake-up time. Gets dressed rapidly. Skips breakfast, thinking that tee-off time and/or practice time will be missed. Golfer leaves in a rushed and tense state with a worried mind.	Golfer gets out of bed quickly and recognizes that tee-off time may be missed. Calls tournament director at country club, explains problem and asks for a later starting time. Golfer slows down, takes a leisurely shower and eats a nutritious breakfast. Golfer is pleased with self for calling and taking care of problem. Relaxes self and begins to mentally prepare for today's round. Golfer leaves home in a relaxed and confident state, with time to go through warm-up practice and slowly prepare for play.

	Situation	Ineffective Response	Effective Response
3.	10:15 A.M. Arrives at golf course and is told the practice range is closed. No more balls for an hour.	Golfer gets mad and yells at pro. What kind of a jerk would let this happen on the day of a tournament? "This will ruin my round. No way I can play well under these circumstances." Golfer is tense, uptight, and worried about poor play due to lack of warm-up practice. Blood pressure and pulse rate are sky high.	Golfer relaxes and realizes he should be happy over delayed tee-off time. "I have frequently played without hitting practice shots. I'll warm up by stretching, swinging, and mentally rehearsing my swing and strategy. I'll spend extra time on the putting green." Golfer is relaxed and confident about ability to play well. Feels especially good about putting stroke.
4.	At thirteenth hole the wind suddenly starts blowing hard with a slight drizzle coming down.	Golfer upset that he must play in lousy weather while those who played earlier had perfect weather. "There is no way that this is fair. No one could play well in this weather. The wind is right in your face on all of the closing holes." Golfer is tense and emotionally upset. Mind is distracted. Starts overswinging and gripping club too tightly.	Golfer realizes that he is lucky to even be playing. Many others are playing in this weather also. "If I can control my head better than others this weather may give me an edge over the golfers who hit the ball better. This is the opportunity I needed. Be sure to adjust club selection to the conditions, swing smoothly, and concentrate on target. If I make a mistake, don't let it cause me to make another one. Stay under control." Golfer is mentally and emotionally controlled and ready to play well despite the weather.
5.	Perfectly hit the shot, straight down the middle, lands in a divot.	Golfer gets mad at misfortune. Gets upset at the inconsiderate player who failed to try and fix divot. "This is just my luck. I never get a break. There is no way I can get this shot to the green out of this lie." Golfer tenses hands, arms, and	Golfer realizes that this is the first bad break he's had today. Stays calm. "If I can handle this I'll be in good shape. It's a good thing I've practiced this shot. I must keep my grip light, and slightly adjust my ball position. If I do these things

A GOLFER'S MIND AND BODY IN ACTION—*Cont.*

Golf Related Situation: (Potential Source of Stress)	Golfing Potential Minimizer: (Copes with Stress Ineffectively)	Golfing Potential Maximizer: (Copes with Stress Effectively)
	shoulders in preparation. Overswings, as a result of negative thoughts and hits shot poorly, resulting in more trouble.	and think target, this shot is not difficult." Golfer stays under control. Swings smoothly and hits good shot. Golfer's shot ends up just short of green in position for par or easy bogey at worst.
6. Eighteenth green surrounded by friends and gallery. Five foot putt needed to qualify for championship flight.	Golfer gets nervous and begins to worry about missing *easy* putt in front of everyone and embarrassing self. "I seem to always miss these putts when I need them. I wish I knew which way this putt would break. I'd like to be aggressive but if I do miss I might three-putt from here and really mess up. I've got to putt and get it over with." Golfer is nervous and tight. Fails to think target. Rushes putt and quits on stroke. Face flushes with embarrassment. Emotionally upset and wonders why he even bothers playing in these tournaments.	Golfer gets nervous and begins worrying about the importance of upcoming putt. But takes a deep slow breath and relaxes self with skills he has developed. "Remember to take my time. Do my routine. Carefully decide on break and speed. 'Feel and 'see' the putt going in before stroking it. Think positively and think target." Golfer is controlled and concentrating. Putt is stroked exactly the way rehearsed and desired. If plan was correct, putt is made. If not, putt is just missed. *Either way golfer is pleased that plan was executed correctly and knows that next time it will drop because he is in control.*

Get up in the morning and let only positive, confidence-inducing thoughts enter your mind. If negative thoughts creep in, stop them and say positive things to yourself. Before each shot on the practice tee, think as if you were on the course. Go through the routine described earlier. Get the feel of a smooth swing. Decide how you will hit your first shot. Plot your strategy and don't change your mind when you get on the first tee.

Once out on the course, stay in control. Use your planned routine and play each shot one at a time. Forget the past or future as you prepare to hit the ball.

After your round, go to the locker room, take a shower, and use the time to prepare yourself. Relax, and as unemotionally as possible, replay your round of golf. Admit your mistakes and then correct them in your mind before leaving the shower. Recall situations that distracted you mentally. Remember your emotional responses, so that if faced with the situation tomorrow, you will be prepared to cope with it and concentrate. Then get dressed and forget about your golf for a while. Self-discipline yourself. Talk with friends, listen to them, watch television, read, listen to music—whatever will relax you and get your mind off your game.

When you feel ready, go to bed. Once again, go through the relaxation exercises and then induce positive self-statements and positive imagery. Think only positive and relaxing thoughts. Drift off to sleep. You are ready to play another greater round of golf tomorrow!

PHYSICAL EFFECTS OF ANXIETY

The physiological effects of anxiety and the "fight or flight" response have already been described. In addition, the possible benefits of calling on adrenalin at just the right time have been described. For most golfers, anxiety is detrimental to their golf score. Let's look at some of the ways this might happen.

Lack of "Feel" and Coordination. Anxiety leads to muscle tension beyond appropriate levels. Suddenly the golfer finds that a usually smooth and coordinated swing becomes quick and uncoordinated. The simultaneous contraction of agonistic, and relaxation of antagonistic, muscles no longer automatically takes place. For example, due to the inability to relax antagonistic muscles you cannot completely extend body parts that normally extend easily when they are relaxed. Thus you lose your follow-through and relaxed finish.

Because of the decrease in blood flow to the fingers and hands when tight, the anxious golfer loses that all-important feel that has been emphasized by so many great golf instructors. Instead you grip the club with the classic death grip so hazardous to your golf swing. Without feel, you suddenly lose rhythm and touch on approach shots and putts. In other words, anxiety prevents your body from doing what it knows how to do.

When your mind remains anxious, your pulse rate increases, your breathing becomes short, shallow, and quick, and you may even become nauseous. Any of these responses, depending upon their degree, may either help or hinder your golf game. The eventual effect on performance is a very individual matter.

When you are anxious, you may realize it and perceive it to mean that you are "psyched up" and ready to perform, or you might perceive it to mean that you are "psyched out" and anxious or "in big trouble." So clearly, your interpretation of your own arousal level makes an important difference.

Recently, an article written in *Sports Illustrated* about Arnold Palmer and the British Open emphasized the importance of self-perception on performance. Palmer had to play on a very wet and cold day. Rather than let these conditions destroy his head and then his game, Palmer decided everyone else had to play in the same conditions. He perceived that he could control his mind and play well despite the conditions, so he had an advantage over many others. Arnold Palmer's perception allowed him to turn the weather conditions into a positive confidence-inducing factor, rather than a negative excuse-generating factor. Your perception of certain situations is very important. It is up to you to perceive things in a helpful way.

Your perception is influenced by several factors. Past experiences, controllability, fatigue, and perceived anxiety or importance of a "round" all effect your perception.

Past Experience. Your past experiences in certain golfing situations will greatly influence your response to physiological arousal. Fortunately, if you just respond to your past experiences, and you have been successful, you will likely interpret arousal in a self-enhancing manner. You will respond with confidence, control your arousal, and perform quite well. However, if you merely respond to your past experiences and they have been negative, you will most likely respond in a self-defeating manner. You may get anxious, increase your arousal level, get overaroused, and perform poorly. This is an important reason why you must learn to implement the coping strategies outlined earlier.

Controllability. Do you see the task before you as controllable or uncontrollable? You must realize that the perception of controllability is quite different from actually being in control. Far too many golfers possess the skills to be in control, but do not believe it. How often do you go into matches deciding ahead of time whether or not you will win? These perceptions greatly influence your arousal level and your performance. Too often golfers interpret situations which they have the skills to control, as being uncontrollable. To do so will greatly limit you, and prevent you from performing up to your potential. It will lead to increased anxiety and decreased motivation.

Fatigue. Because your muscles tend to stay tense for prolonged periods and at inappropriate times, you will be much more susceptible to fatigue. When you are tired, you will not be able to cope with stress as effectively. For this reason, plenty of rest and keeping yourself physically fit are important to your ability to face stress effectively. Do you ever find that your shoulders and upper back are sore after playing? They will certainly tire easily if they never relax and recover. Combine this problem with the already discussed "fight or flight" effects on the breathing process and you quickly understand the problem and why you may also be more susceptible to injury. Suddenly it becomes clear that good golfers know what they are doing when they take deep, slow breaths and concentrate on relaxing their shoulders between shots and prior to planning and hitting shots.

As is obvious by this point, anxiety is not good for your game. You must be aware of your anxiety-related tendencies and understand their relationship to performance. Finally, and of equal if not more importance, is the understanding that anxiety is learned and therefore you can learn to control and eliminate it.

ASSESSING YOUR OWN LEVEL OF ANXIETY TO INCREASE SELF-AWARENESS

A very simple and yet effective method of assessing anxiety in golf is to become more self-aware of your thinking style. Because anxiety is a psychological state, one's thinking as well as physiological responses (arousal) will tell you a great deal about whether or not you're anxious or self-confident. Following your next important round of golf, sit down in a quiet place and answer the following questions as honestly as possible.

1. What were your self thoughts the day before the match? Did you fully expect to win or play well? Did you often have negative thoughts cross your mind? Were you worried about a particular shot or hole that has given you trouble in the past? Did you

worry that the wind would be blowing and you would play poorly? Did you fear that your wedge would fail you?

(Write down your thoughts as you remember them. The anxious thoughts suggest that you need to spend more time in the future on both physical and mental practice on those aspects of your game. If you lacked confidence, more needs to be done with your self-efficacy training).

2. When did you feel the most anxious? On deck on the first tee? After going out of bounds on the third hole? Were you positive that you could recover or did you question your ability to do so? What did you say to yourself prior to the six-footer on eighteen for the match? Did you worry about missing it? Were you wondering what your friends or partner would think if you missed or made it?

If you can become increasingly self-aware of these specific problem areas you will be better able to apply the mastery and coping rehearsal where they are most necessitated.

If possible, it can be quite effective to videotape your play on a number of holes or situations. Then play back the tape and while viewing yourself, record your inner thoughts. Again, the key is to want to understand your mental deficiencies, realize that they *can* be improved, and use the described techniques to do so.

6
Eliminating Inappropriate
Muscle Tension

Many golfers fail to understand the detrimental effects of inappropriate muscle tension, or lack knowledge concerning what to do about it. Much too often its effects are not even considered.

Many golf instructors will emphasize the importance of the contraction of certain muscle groups which are required to execute the golf swing. However, far too many golfers are hurt by contracting these muscles too tightly with the result of ineffective and inconsistent performance. Unfortunately, most golfers are at a loss when it comes time to eliminate the excess tension. Frequently our only response is to yell at ourselves, "R-E-L-A-X." Naturally because we have not practiced how to do so and are well aware that we can't control it, our brain sends messages to the body indicating anxiety which only increases muscle tension rather than decreasing it.

Any time a golf swing is executed there are two muscle groups which must be controlled for a smooth, coordinated movement. Too frequently we concern ourselves with the main mover known as the agonistic muscles. But in order to have a coordinated and efficient swing the opposite muscle group (the antagonists) must simultaneously relax. Unfortunately, when we "choke" in golf, it is usually the result of the golfer's inability to identify and control inappropriate muscle tension.

It is important for golfers to gauge their own body tension. The following questions were formulated to guide your practice.

SELF-ASSESSMENT TEST FOR GAUGING BODY TENSION

Instructions: Circle the response which best describes your response to the situation described next to it.

Behavior	Strongly Agree	Agree	Disagree	Strongly Disagree
1. When I finish playing a round of competitive golf, I have sore shoulders and/or neck.	4	3	2	1
2. During a round of golf I have nervous indigestion.	4	3	2	1
3. I have tension or migraine headaches prior to, during, or following a competitive match.	4	3	2	1
4. I have insomnia the night before and/or after a competitive golf match.	4	3	2	1
5. I have difficulty relaxing my hands on important shots.	4	3	2	1
6. I feel that I get more tired than I should during tournament play.	4	3	2	1
7. I find myself holding my breath on important shots.	4	3	2	1
8. During tournaments I find that I sweat profusely.	4	3	2	1
9. In tournament play my legs don't seem to work for me as well as they normally do.	4	3	2	1
10. I eat/smoke/drink in response to tension.	4	3	2	1

Scoring: Add the total for your responses

Maximum Score $=$ 40   My Total Score $=$ _____

Zone	Score	Tension Level
A	40–36	Considerably Above Average
B	35–29	Above Average
C	28–21	Average
D	20–14	Below Average
E	13–10	Considerably Below Average

If you determine from your self-assessment test that you have an above-average level of body tension, relax. There are many techniques which you will learn through this book that will greatly improve your golf as well as reduce your general stress level.

BREATH CONTROL: THE MOST SIMPLE AND NATURAL RELAXATION CONTROL MECHANISM

The fact that the whole concept of tightness during performance can be identified by the term "choke" (which relates to breathing) tells you something about the importance of breath control. Master performers of the martial arts have understood the relevance of breathing control to tension management. Certainly in recent years, anyone familiar with the "Lamaze" natural childbirth techniques realizes the value of breath control to muscle relaxation. This technique can facilitate relaxation and exercise control over the "fight or flight" syndrome.

A deep, slow breath in a stressful situation tells the brain that the body is back in control. The result may yield a reduction in the "fight or flight" response, which may naturally lead to increased muscle relaxation.

Many successful golfers have learned to prevent excess tension by simply taking a couple of deep, slow breaths any time they anticipate a stressful situation. Take a deep, slow breath yourself and feel the relaxed feeling that comes over your body during and following exhalation. This is the reason that the relaxed golfer should continue to breathe during execution of the golf swing, and perhaps even experiment with the effects of a *smile* on relaxation.

It is well recognized that because of the increased relaxed state resulting from a forced exhalation, the distance of your drives can be increased. This certainly explains the cries and yells in many of the martial arts at delivery of a blow. Many golfers who have tended to hold their breath in the past may immediately experience an increase in distance of five to nine yards from simply breathing out on the downswing and finishing in the contact area. A normal breath is most desirable, however, for most golf shots.

A final point should be emphasized. The benefit of controlled breathing will not be realized while you are thinking about doing so. It must become an automatic behavior and will with practice and relaxation.

DIFFERENTIATING BETWEEN COMPLETE AND DIFFERENTIAL RELAXATION

Mastering the game of golf requires not only mastery of muscle contraction, but also mastery of muscle relaxation. Indeed, it is the correct differential relaxation that distinguishes the skillful golfer from the uncoordinated one. As a matter of fact, coordination may be defined in correct differential relaxation. The swing of the poor golfer suffers from either (1) contracting too forcefully muscles requiring some degree of tension, or (2) contracting muscles which should be relaxed to produce a smooth golf swing.

It is helpful to understand the difference between complete and differential relaxation. Complete relaxation means zero activity of the voluntary muscles of the body. The normal tension of the muscles will be absent in appearance. Complete muscle relaxation is extremely useful for inducing sleep and for gaining greater self-awareness of muscle relaxation. Differential relaxation means differentiating between muscles that are necessary for an activity, such as golf, and those that are not. To relax muscles that are not needed in the performance of the golf swing, (e.g., or a tee shot, sand shot, putting stroke) or while walking down the fairway, is differential relaxation. It also means differentiating between strong and weak contractions of the required muscles and relaxing them as much as is consistent with doing the job in hand effectively. Thus for mastery of golf, differential relaxation should be practiced continually in conjunction with a wide variety of daily activities, as well as with the movements demanded in golf.

ALTERNATE RELAXATION AND CONCENTRATION

The ability to totally concentrate, alternated with relaxation is one of the keys to good golf. No one can effectively concentrate one hundred percent of the time during a round of golf. Let us assume that within the four hours required to play eighteen holes of golf, it takes less than half that time to actually mentally prepare and physically execute the shot. The implication here is obvious. During fifty percent of your time on the course you should be moderately relaxed.

The ability to accept reality may be the key to relaxation. Recognize that you cannot change what already exists during a match. If your ball is already out of bounds, don't "stew" over that fact and berate yourself. Accept it, and decide on the *next* shot. Having confidence in your ability and looking forward are critical.

The concept of relaxation does not, on the other hand, suggest a fatalistic attitude toward your game, or the strategy of diverted attention. Nothing can be worse for your game than thinking about your business or family affairs while on the course. Unresolved problems or unfinished projects place a tremendous stress on your ability to concentrate and relax. It is therefore critical that you give yourself time to resolve problems, or at least "shift gears" before you begin your round of golf.

INCREASING SENSITIVITY

The first phase of learning to relax while playing golf is to increase your self-awareness of the difference between various degrees of muscle relaxation and tension. Clearly, in order to eliminate tension you must increase your sensitivity to it in order to better recognize it and then control it. The following exercises have been developed to help in this process. As you practice them, feel for areas of your body where you have the most difficulty eliminating tension. These areas may require special practice because it is most likely they will cause problems in your golf swing.

COMPLETE BODY RELAXATION
EXERCISES

Find a quiet place where you can lie down for about fifteen to twenty minutes each day for the next two weeks. Lie down on your back and make yourself comfortable. (You may wish to place a pillow under your neck and/or the back of your knees.) Place your arms at your sides, with your fingers open. Close your eyes comfortably—don't squeeze your eyelids tightly.

While practicing the following exercises, focus your attention on the way your body feels. If your mind wanders onto other thoughts, calmly tell yourself "STOP," push them away, and concentrate on your bodily feelings.

These exercises have two major functions: (1) to increase your recognition and awareness of muscle tension and relaxation and (2) to increase your ability to eliminate muscle tension and induce muscle relaxation.

Lie down (sit if you cannot lie) in a quiet and comfortable place. Close your eyes. Do not force them shut. Hold them comfortably closed. Tense all of the muscles in the lower part of your body from your hips to the tip of your toes. Point your toes away from your body with your heels about four to six inches apart. Tighten the muscles in your calves, thighs, buttocks. Feel the tension as you hold it. Remember this feeling. 1 . . . 2 . . . 3 . . . 4 . . . Repeat the words "let go" to yourself and slowly let the tension flow out of your body. Again concentrate on calves, thighs, buttocks. Let your toes point upward and flop to the outside. Feel the relaxation. Remember how good it feels. Feel the heaviness and the warmth flowing through the lower body. Let it feel good. If you have any tension anywhere in your lower body, "let go."

Now concentrate on your stomach. Tighten as much as you can. Feel the tension as you hold it. Remember the feeling. 1 . . . 2 . . . 3 . . . 4 . . . Repeat the words "let go" to yourself and slowly let the tension flow out of your body. Again, concentrate on your stomach muscles. Feel the relaxation. Remember how good it feels. Let it feel good for a moment. If there is any tension anywhere in your body, let it go.

Concentrate on your chest muscles. Tighten your chest muscles as tightly as you can. Take a deep breath through your mouth and then hold it. As you hold it you may feel tension spots in your chest. Remember where they are— they may surface on the golf course. Now slowly "let go"— very slowly. Breathe normally and comfortably as if you were sleeping or resting. Make sure you have eliminated the tension spots. Relax your whole body completely.

Tighten all of the muscles, from the tips of your fingers to your shoulders, in both arms as tightly as you can. Raise your arms about one foot off the floor. Clench your fists. Feel the tension throughout your fingers, hands, arms, and shoulders. Hold it. 1 . . . 2 . . . 3 . . . 4 . . . and feel the tension. Slowly "let go." Let your arms drop, your fingers spread and completely relax. Feel your hands and arms. If there is any remaining tension, remember where it is. You are likely to get tension there while playing golf in a stressful situation. Now, "let go" and completely relax.

Once again, concentrate on just your fingers. Relax them completely. Feel how warm and heavy they are. Relax your upper arms completely. Eliminate any excess tension.

Now concentrate on the muscles of your upper back— the muscles between the shoulder blades and the neck. These muscles are very sensitive to tension. You may have experienced soreness here after a tournament. Tighten these muscles as much as possible. Feel the tension and hold it. 1 . . . 2 . . . 3 . . . 4 . . . Slowly "let go." Dwell on the feelings of relaxation as you do so. Concentrate on these relaxed feelings and remember them.

Now tighten your entire body as tightly as you can from the tips of your fingers to the top of your toes. Hold it. 1 . . . 2 . . . 3 . . . 4 . . . Slowly "let go" and completely relax your entire body. If you have any residual tension remaining anywhere in your body, let it go.

If there are any places in your body where you have a tendency to get tension, eliminate them.

Imagine a pleasant scene, like walking on a beach, lying in a row boat on a calm pond—any place that you feel completely relaxed. Let your whole body feel calm and relaxed. Enjoy the feelings. Take a couple of very deep, slow breaths. Inhale deeply into your stomach—1 . . . 2 . . . 3 . . . 4 . . . and then exhale slowly—1 . . . 2 . . . 3 . . . 4 . . . Feel your body get more and more relaxed. Breathe normally, smoothly, and calmly. Continue to feel your body and let go any remaining tension.

Differential Relaxation Techniques

1. Focus your attention on your right arm and contract the muscles of your arm and wrist. Make a fist. Do an isometric contraction without moving, from the shoulder to the tips of your fingers. Keep all of the other muscles of your body relaxed—legs, left arm, breathe normally. As you tense the right side, feel the difference between the right and left side of your body. Feel your legs. Do you have any tension remaining in your legs? If you do, let it go. Keep the whole body relaxed while maintaining a tense right arm. 1 . . . 2 . . . 3 . . . 4 . . . 5. Now relax your right arm also. That's it. Let the whole body feel good and relax. Keep breathing.

2. Repeat the same process, but this time tighten the muscles of your left arm and hand, totally relax the rest of your body.

3. Focus your attention on your left arm and your right leg. Tighten

them as tightly as you can while keeping all of the other muscles of your body completely relaxed. Feel your body. . . . Is there tension in your right arm? Let it go completely. Is there any tension in your left leg? Let it go completely.

Gradually let the tension go in your left arm and right leg. Stop at different degrees of tension along the way. Keep the left arm and right leg one-half tense while relaxing all other muscles totally. Now one-third tense. Keep on breathing smoothly and rhythmically. Now relax the whole body.

4. Focus your attention on the three small fingers on both your right and left hand. Squeeze these fingers into the palm of your hand. Keep the index finger and thumb of each hand totally relaxed. Feel your hands. If there is still tension in the index finger or thumb, let it go. Feel your lower and upper arm. Feel your bicep and tricip. Are they relaxed or is there tension? Let some of the tension go in your little fingers. A little more. Imagine you are holding a baby bird or a tube of toothpaste with your little fingers. Keep the rest of your body relaxed.

   Now totally relax your whole body.

5. Focus your attention on your shoulders. Shrug both of your shoulders up toward your ears. Keep them there. Feel the tension in the back of your shoulders. Totally relax the rest of your body. Continue to breathe smoothly and regularly. Slowly release the tension in your shoulders and relax your whole body.

   Now shrug your shoulders up to your ears again, while keeping the rest of your body relaxed. Relax and lower your right shoulder only. Completely relax the right shoulder while maintaining tension in the left. Focus on the relaxed feelings in the left shoulder and the tension in your right shoulder.

6. Focus your attention on your left shoulder. Raise it slightly and feel the tension in the back of your left shoulder. Completely relax your right shoulder and the rest of your body. Breathe smoothly and regularly. 1 . . . 2 . . . 3 . . . 4 . . . 5 . . . Slowly let go and relax your whole body.

7. Stretch your whole body slowly. Open your eyes and stand up. Assume your golf stance. Place your club in your hands. Grip the club in your hands. Grip the club lightly with slight pressure in the three small fingers of each hand. Feel a little more pressure on the target left fingers than in the rear hand. Remember to keep the thumbs and index finger completely relaxed.

7
Getting the Most Out of Your Practice

*Practice Doesn't Make Perfect,
Only Perfect Practice Makes Perfect.*

Now that you have decided you will work to improve your weaknesses and perfect your strengths, you are ready to read and better understand the rest of this book. You are willing to become increasingly self-aware of the mental side of your game. You have selected the best teacher available. You have had a lesson, or many lessons. How do you now combine physical and mental practice in a way that is most effective for attaining success? Remember—if you are going to practice, make sure your practice is designed to maximize your payoff—improvement and success in golf.

Right from the very start you should practice in a manner conducive to the formation of good habits. Habits do not change easily, and are rather stable, even under pressure situations. Of course, if you form *bad* habits this point also holds true. Bad habits are difficult to change. If you establish no set practice pattern, you will not form habits at all, and will be likely to have problems in stressful situations.

When you arrive at the practice tee, begin with your standard routine. Loosen up and do the flexibility exercises discussed earlier. Take a couple of deep, slow breaths and mentally go through your practice plan and goals. It is important at this time to imagine your planned practice paying off and helping you to be successful. Do not allow any negative or self-defeating thoughts such as, "What am I doing out here while others are inside drinking or taking it easy?" enter your mind. You have made a commitment to attain a certain goal—stick with your practice plan to reach it— be persistent.

CONCENTRATE: IT TAKES
SELF-DISCIPLINE

From the moment your practice session starts to the moment it ends, be sure that you concentrate. Don't let yourself quickly hit a hundred practice balls. Slow down, analyze, and go through your complete pre-swing, swing, and post-swing routine, always using a target and real or imagined boundaries. Do not allow a sloppy day of practice. Start learning and preparing for matches and plan how to control your arousal level. If you are tired and bored in practice, learn how to get yourself up and ready. If you start hitting the ball poorly and you feel yourself getting anxious and distracted, practice controlling the focus of your attention. Get your confidence back, breathe deeply, relax, go through your routine, and hit.

Most golfers who have put some thought into their golf game realize they may hit the ball slightly different on certain days. Start to recognize these tendencies. What happens when you are tired? How about when you feel strong? As you learn to recognize these tendencies, experiment with correcting them. Know that you can self-correct them when they occur in any round of golf.

Play Mind Games

Have you ever closely observed the golf of players who are tournament tough? Watch how people who love competition enjoy playing "mind games" throughout their daily practice rounds. "Mind games" are those verbal challenges that golfers make to each other. The intent is usually to emotionally upset and distract a person's mind from the task at hand. Often, when other less competitive golfers observe their behavior, they perceive these people as being sick and cruel. They can't understand how anyone could be so unsportsmanlike. This is very different from the perception of those playing the mind games. The players are simply preparing themselves for the mental and physical challenges likely to be present during intense competition. They are quite aware of the importance of preparing ahead of time how to control emotional responses and learn to concentrate.

Due to their very different perception of the challenges presented, tournament players *enjoy* "mind games." They interpret them as learning experiences that can help them improve their performance in tournaments. They recognize that to avoid them would be foolish. They realize that such "mind games" will help point out their weaknesses while there still is time to improve. They realize that by increasing their self-awareness they can learn to improve their self-control and become more consistent tournament performers.

CHALLENGE YOUR MIND

Try these Mind Games on the practice tee:

—Hit low iron shots to targets with the ball sitting down in a divot.

—Hit practice balls on an extremely windy day. Practice hitting shots with the wind blowing in all different directions—directly in your face, at your back, and across your body from either side.

—Purposely hit ten consecutively practice shots poorly. Try to lose your rhythm. Swing quickly, jump, swing from the top, lose your balance, quit on a shot. Stop and try and immediately get your rhythm and confidence back. Swing smoothly.

—Practice hitting shots off uncomfortable lies: steep uphill, downhill, and sidehill lies.

—Hit practice shots out of a sand trap: try buried and partially buried lies, uphill and downhill lies. Also try wet sand and heavy sand.

—Practice on an extremely hot and humid day and on extremely cold days.

—Try to hit practice shots for four consecutive hours without losing your concentration. Hit every shot with your routine.

—Hit ten consecutive putts from a distance of three feet, attempting to push or pull each of them. Stop and try to immediately get your stroke back and concentrate on the hole.

—Practice hitting shots out of deep rough (with or against you), off hard pan, off wood chips, and/or off a wet, soft surface.

—Practice hitting fades, slices, draw hooks, duck hooks, and shanks. Try to constantly change and then hit ten straight shots in a row.

—Practice hitting pitch shots over a sand trap to a tightly cut pin. Challenge yourself by quitting on the shot and putting the ball in the sand and then see if you can hit ten effective shots in a row.

—Practice putting or chipping with tough breaks competitively. Bet with others and make dares. Play psych-out games where anything goes. Learn to handle any form of distraction that could interfere with your confidence and concentration on or around the green.

Try these Mind Games during practice rounds:

—Have your partner and opponents talk while you are hitting your shots.

—Have your partner and opponents drop a ball or club when you are hitting your shots.

—Have your partner and opponents verbally taunt you just prior to hitting a shot. The following are some examples:

Suggest you are going to hit OB.

Tell you your swing looks terrible.

Ask you why you can't hit the ball any farther than you do.

Remind you that a shank would put you in the water and ruin a good round.

Remind you that three pars on the finishing holes would give you a personal best round ever.

—Make it acceptable for your partners to move while you are swinging.

—Tell your partners that anything except physically interfering with your swing is legal.

—Create your own ideas and challenges.*

MODEL TRAINING

As you start getting your swing grooved, start to utilize the concept known as model training—start to simulate the competitive situation in your practice sessions. Begin to change clubs with each practice shot in a sequence similar to that likely to occur on the course. Practice bad lies, getting out of divots, rough, downhill, uphill, sidehill, pine nee-

---

* Remember that the idea of these games is to prepare you for competition. Enjoy them and learn from your mistakes. DO NOT GET UPSET BY THEM. If you do at first, recognize it as a response weakness that you must learn to control. REALIZE THAT IF YOU HAVE TO YOU CAN CONCENTRATE AND PERFORM UNDER ANY CONDITION. If you recognize and attend to the distractor, learn to discipline yourself to stop your swing, start your routine over again, and then hit. But also see if you can get so good at concentration that you don't even notice or attend to the distractor. Keep in mind this point: The time to learn and grow is in *PRACTICE*.

dles, wood chips, dirt roads. Hit into the wind, with the wind, in cross winds. Instead of skipping practice on rainy days, dress to be warm and dry and go out and learn to hit well in the wet. Do the same on cold and hot days. Study the flight of the ball in these various situations and record the information in your brain. For particularly important facts, record them in a little book you can always carry with you. Be sure you have also recorded in detail your distance for each club. Do you tend to hit a low or high ball? How will this affect your distance on windy days?

PREPARE FOR THE MATCH

Induce anxiety and distractions into your practice sessions. Set up contests with an opponent, with the loser picking up the balls. During the contest have your opponent make noises, make unexpected movements, make you feel self-conscious by describing how your swing looks as you're about to hit. You'll be amazed at how well you can learn to hit despite these distractions.

As the competitive event draws near, it is best to emphasize confidence development in both your physical and mental practice. If you haven't mastered it by now, forget it until after the match. On the last two days of preparation, do everything possible to increase the likelihood of hitting only good shots. Spend extra time on building confidence in your putting, pitching, and chipping. Practice lots of short, easy putts and chips that are likely to drop. Again, take your time and concentrate as you practice. Mentally imagine and feel only perfect shots. Visualize successful results. Imagine arriving at the match, signing in, practicing, and playing always with successful results. Do not allow anxieties or self-doubts to cross your mind.

Play the match and do your best—always go through your routine and control your attention as you know you should.

At the end of each round, analyze your mistakes or bad shots and mentally correct them. Before going to sleep, visually imagine playing the course perfectly and go to sleep ready to do your best tomorrow. If you are in the lead, don't allow unnecessary pressures to enter your mind. Remember, concentration is thinking in the present, not in the past or future. If you find yourself thinking about blowing and being considered a "choker," or fearing that if you win you'll have more pressure to win again, recognize these thoughts as anxieties and distractions and induce relaxation. Continue to work with positive imagery to calm your mind and to get the proper frame of mind back again.

POST-TOURNAMENT EVALUATION

Lie down. Think through your play during the tournament. Once again, list your strengths and weaknesses. Get ready to go back to work on the weaknesses so that you can eliminate them. Did you get anxious? Tight? Could you control your attention? Did you go through your routine on all shots or did you forget at crucial times as a result of stress?

Realize that the mere fact that you are now recognizing these problems will help you to become a success. Be confident that you will.

USING YOUR LAST ROUND OF GOLF TO DIRECT YOUR PRACTICE

Each time you play a round of golf, you should use it to indicate the relative strengths and weaknesses of your game. It is important that you have an outward focus during the round, but that after each experience, you analyze your performance and plan the subsequent practices in relation to your strengths and weaknesses.

One useful technique is to carefully evaluate each round of golf, each hole for that matter, in relation to your individual strengths and weaknesses. Analyze each stroke utilized in terms of the appropriate club selection as well as the execution. For example, the self-performance chart introduced on page 22 may be useful, and perhaps Tom's example on page 104 will help illustrate this point.

For each hole, he recorded the clubs selected and the resultant physical and mental performance for each stroke. That is, he indicated the first club selected, and the outcome of the swing (for example, good distance, sliced). Tom did the same for each club until the end of the round. He then summarized the performance and used the results to indicate his next practice concentration.

The following golf profile illustrates the relative strengths and weaknesses of our golf friend, Tom. Note that when Tom played at Westwoods, his middle irons were his most reliable shots. He was able to demonstrate complete mental concentration (CMC), and his shots were generally on target. In contrast, his ability to drive well and play his woods consistently was impacted by his excess body tension (BT) and negative thinking (NT).

Tom's evaluation of his own play can now guide the focus of his practice sessions. He has identified the following goals for at least the next thirty days of practice:

Physical Aspects: Hit twenty drives with No. 1 and 3 woods
                  Practice putting from twenty feet or more
Mental Aspects: Utilize techniques of positive thinking
                  Practice relaxation techniques

These practice goals are quite different than his previous concentration on the midirons, which were his most reliable shots.

This analysis of Tom's round of golf showed him several patterns within his play. In particular, the seventeen instances of negative thinking, which generally occurred dur-

NAME: _Tom_ COURSE: _Westwoods_

DATE: _April 8_

SELF PERFORMANCE CHART

Hole	Yards	PAR	Woods 1	Woods 2	Woods 3	Woods 4	Woods 5	Irons 1	Irons 2	Irons 3	Irons 4	Irons 5	Irons 6	Irons 7	Irons 8	Irons 9	Wedge	Greens hit in Regulation	Putts 1st	Putts 2nd	Putts 3rd
1	375	4	R BT											RO NT			O FR		u FR	√ CC	
2	172	3		√ CC														ok	CC		
3	391	4	√ CC							√ CC								ok	u UA	√ CC	
4	351	4			L OA							√ CC						ok	O NT	√ CC	
5	419	4	√ NT		RO NT										u FR				u NT	√ BT	
6	154	3				R BT							√ CC				√ CC	ok	u NT	√ CC	
7	513	5	R OA			R BT								√ NT					LU NT	O NT	√ BT
8	387	4	R NT		R UA										√ CC			ok	√ CC	√ CC	
9	340	4														√ CC			O NT	NT NT	√ CC
10	216	3	LU NT														u UA	ok	u BT	√ CC	
11	418	4	u NT			√ CC													√ UA	√ LA	√ BT
12	315	4	R NT											√ CC				ok	u UA	√ CC	
13	360	4	L BT		RO NT										√ CC		u UA	ok	R NT	√ CC	
14	449	4	L BT							R NT					√ CC				R CC	√ CC	
15	340	4	L OA			L FR												ok	R NT	√ CC	
16	537	5	√ CC													√ CC	√ CC	ok	√ NT	√ CC	
17	154	3									√ CC							ok	R uA	R uA	
18	391	4	√ CC									√ CC						ok	R uA	√ LA	

Physical Aspects:
√ = on target
s = sliced
h = hooked
o = beyond target
u = short of target

MENTAL ASPECTS:
NT = Negative Thinking
LA = Lack of Attentional control
BT = Excess Body Tension
FR = Failure to use Routine

OA = Over Aroused
UA = Under Aroused
CC = Complete Mental Control

Summary

Physical Aspects:

√ = 36

R = 16

L = 7

O = 7

U = 12

Mental Aspects:

NT = 19

LA = 2

BT = 7

FR = 5

OA = 3

UA = 6

CC = 31

ing his putts or wood shots, strongly influenced his re-defin-
ing of practice goals. He may also wish to attend (at a later
date) to a slight alignment problem which biased sixteen
of his shots to the right, as compared to seven to the left,
and a difficulty with force control on putts that left nine
early putts short of the hole compared to three putts which
went beyond the target.

If, after careful self-direction, you are not fully certain
that you are working on improving your skills in the most
effective manner, find a knowledgeable friend, or prefer-
ably a qualified golf instructor, who can help you. A good
instructor can help your game and your head by instilling
confidence and helping you focus on the important aspects
of your golf game.

8
Getting the Most
Out of Your Golf Lesson

The key to *Mastering Your Mind for Winning Golf* is a consistent approach to your game. This consistency is affected by your ability to direct your own practices, and by the ability of others to reinforce your strengths while simultaneously working on your weaknesses. A good instructor can greatly enhance the efficiency of your game. Unfortunately, because of various psychological barriers, many golf students never get their money's worth out of a lesson. Often the problems are caused by personality or communication deficits on the part of the instructor. If you hear from others that certain pros have such problems, and you are sure that the information is accurate, then don't waste your money or your time on them.

But what about the commonly occurring situation where the psychological or communication barriers are due to you. Perhaps you go to your first lesson feeling that you are a lousy golfer. You are quite shy and self-conscious as you approach the practice tee. You start to hit a few shots to show the pro that you really are a good golfer. But you are trying too hard and start spraying your shots all over the place. Pretty soon you are embarrassed. You begin to imagine that the pro hates teaching such an incompetent student. Despite your teacher's good intentions to show you your problems and correct them, you are not really listening. You are more intent on showing the instructor that you really are a good golfer. Your lesson ends, you pay the pro and go home. The next morning you head to the practice tee. You discover that you learned nothing at your lesson. That does it. Lessons are useless. You decide to never take another.

If this reminds you of someone you know rather well, it is time for a change. Most golfers have the physical ability required but are not good enough students to become low-handicap golfers. It would be very difficult to identify many golfers on the pro tour who have not had lessons, or who do not still take lessons on occasion. When a playing professional takes a lesson, the anxieties experienced by the average or weekend golfer are usually absent or greatly reduced. But even at the professional level there are golfers who are not playing up to their potential because they either don't hear, or don't wish to hear the instructions. If you take a lesson, decide to accept what the teacher suggests. Resist the temptation to be defensive or feel that the pro's decisions are not worthwhile.

PICKING AN EFFECTIVE TEACHER

Try to find out as much as possible about the available teachers before ever taking a lesson. Talk to others who have taken lessons from them. Whenever possible, get permission to observe the prospective teacher in action. A good teacher will not be reluctant to allow you to watch, unless you may bother the present student. So make sure that you are concerned about the student taking the lesson. Do not distract his/her attention, or that of the teacher. Stand back out of the way and simply observe and think. Would you enjoy taking a lesson from this teacher? Does the instructor appear to have a thorough understanding of the skills of golf? Is the teacher organized and prepared? Does the teacher effectively communicate knowledge to the student? Is the atmosphere relaxed and conducive to learning? Or does the teacher like to destroy confidence and show off? When the teacher demonstrates correct execution of shots, is attention placed on the pertinent body parts of the instructor

or the golf club? Or is the student allowed to continually watch only how far and straight the teacher's shots have gone? Is the teacher's main instructional comment, "Keep your head down," or does the teacher really teach?

Possibly the single most important ingredient to look for in a golf teacher, aside from the ability to teach appropriate mechanical skills, is whether he or she builds confidence in each student's ability. Students will become what their teacher expects them to become. Teachers who encourage you by emphasizing that you have ability, will motivate you to practice. Obviously, if you have the ability, all you need to do is practice effectively. However, teachers who tend to tell their students that they are lacking in coordination or strength usually suggest to their students that they should stop practicing. Let's face it, if you have no ability, what good will practice do? Fortunately, most individuals who spend the time and effort to golf, have at least some ability, and the instructor's task then becomes to optimize that ability. It is also important to note that research studies have shown that the perception of one's ability which is communicated to the student is more important to achievement than whether or not the student is actually talented.

Recent research as well as comments by many current professional golfers has made it very clear that teacher expectations have a very significant impact on the future learning and performance of each student. Teachers treat their students very differently based upon their performance expectancies. If a teacher believes that a student has great potential in golf, they give the student more attention and interest. The quality of the attention also tends to be much greater.

It is quite clear that teachers make value judgments about their students. Their teaching style often varies greatly based upon how they view that student's abilities and interests. Students evaluated favorably receive more positive feedback and are often encouraged to practice diligently.

What should be obvious by now is that students frequently become what their teachers expect them to become. Every golfer should be aware of this inclination. Take responsibility for your own future outcomes. If you have a teacher who does not get excited about teaching you and does not see you as having potential, find a new instructor. It is highly likely that your present teacher will not be the best for the future development of your game.

What happens at the end of the lesson? Does the teacher leave you feeling good about the lesson? Does the teacher identify a few key points for the student to practice? Is the student told fairly precisely how to practice? Are there drills described? Is the student asked to attain a certain level of proficiency prior to the next lesson? Does the teacher give the student a form in writing which recaptures the major points of the lesson? Are goals and target skills progressively more difficult, yet held within reach? This will prevent the student from hearing only half of the lesson due to fear of forgetting the last point the teacher made. It will also insure that the key points are not forgotten in the near future.

DO NOT PUT UNNECESSARY PRESSURES ON YOURSELF

Far too many individuals play golf only once or twice a week and imagine that they should be as good as the pros they see on T.V. Many of these golfers take a few lessons from the pro and expect a miracle. This attitude will only tend to make you and your instructor nervous. The result will be a less than effective lesson.

If you find that during the course of your lesson you are not fully comprehending what the teacher is telling you, do not allow yourself to be timid and worried. Speak up. Stop the instructor. Another approach may get the point across. Do not let yourself feel that you are inadequate because you did not understand the teacher. A good teacher will try to find a way to get the message across to you.

PRACTICING AFTER THE LESSON

Following your lessons, it is an excellent idea to take your lesson notes home and review them often. Put them in your golf bag and take them with you to the practice tee.

New golf skills will not be mastered overnight. Patience and practice are the only answers. Do not allow yourself to play in a competitive situation until you are sure you have perfected the new techniques. Competition will most likely lead you to slip back to your old swing with which you still feel more comfortable.

A better idea would be to practice on the range until

you feel comfortable and relaxed with your new swing. Then, try to induce pressure into your practice session on the practice range. Next, go out on the golf course alone with a few balls and try out your new skills. Finally, you should be ready. If you find out that you're not, don't be discouraged. Go back to the practice range and practice some more.

Hopefully, the ideas presented here will help you get more out of those expensive lessons. But let us remind you of one point: You will never "perfect" the game of golf, so don't expect to. Even the great Walter Hagen has stated that he expected to make at least seven bad shots a round. In doing so, he prevented himself from being frustrated when he did so.

Remember—set yourself up for success rather than failure.

9
Playing the Game of Golf

Becoming a relative success on the golf course requires a wide range of physical and mental skills. From a psychological perspective there are several strategies you should be aware of that could greatly benefit your game. These strategies apply to both medal and match play.

Try at all times to play within your own abilities. Know which shots you can execute and which shots you are not so good at. Control how safe or aggressively you play based on the likelihood of being successful. Usually an inclination to play the highest percentage shot rather than take a chance or play boldly will have the greater payoff in golf. But, if you do decide that you need to play aggressively, do so with a shot that has a good chance for success. In other words, be aggressive when necessary and when there is a good chance that you will be rewarded, but do not gamble unwisely or play low-percentage shots.

Prior to stepping up to the first tee, be sure that you are ready and positive. Do not allow yourself to start out filled with fear of losing or looking bad. This approach can only cause you to play "tight" and defensively. Do not become a player that has to be down before getting started. Starting successfully will be a benefit to muscle and mind, it will aid you to relax, and will help your confidence by putting the pressure on the other golfers. Go for pars and gladly take birdies or eagles as a bonus. If you are playing for par on the first hole and you find yourself with a ten-foot birdie putt, be sure to be positive and go for the birdie.

Do not think too safely and merely lag up to the hole. Be confident.

Playing a good round of golf requires that you accurately gauge your own physical abilities as well as your ability to cope with stress. The following self-assessment questionnaire may help you learn more about your playing style.

SELF-SCORING TEST FOR GAUGING STRESS LEVELS IN GOLF

Instructions: Circle the response which most agrees with your response to the situation described next to it.

Situation	Strongly Agree	Agree	Disagree	Strongly Disagree
1. It upsets me when my playing partners show up late for a tee-off time.	4	3	2	1
2. I get upset when the players in front of me play slowly.	4	3	2	1
3. It bothers me to play with others who play faster or slower than I do.	4	3	2	1
4. Players who spend a lot of time looking for "lost balls" make me mad.	4	3	2	1
5. I get upset by players that are never ready to hit their next shot when it is their turn.	4	3	2	1
6. I rush and play poorly when the group behind me pushes.	4	3	2	1
7. I am self-conscious and/or uncomfortable when I play with players who are better than I am.	4	3	2	1
8. It bothers me when players riding in carts want to rush through everyone.	4	3	2	1

Situation	Strongly Agree	Agree	Disagree	Strongly Disagree
9. I often find myself "racing" around the golf course to save time.	4	3	2	1
10. When I play with someone for the first time, I often feel tense and play poorly.	4	3	2	1

Maximum Score = 40   My Total Score _____

Zone	Score	Tension Level
A	40–36	Considerably Above Average
B	35–29	Above Average
C	28–21	Average
D	20–14	Below Average
E	13–10	Considerably Below Average

This self-assessment for stress is particularly helpful as it relates to actually playing the game of golf. As a result of reading the first section of *Mastering Your Mind for Winning Golf*, you have already discovered some important information about your own ability to control stress and anxiety. If your tension levels are average or above average, you should concentrate on reducing stress while golfing.

COACH YOURSELF

On the golf course you are alone. Utilize what you know about the physical and mental side of playing golf. Prepare yourself for success, monitor your arousal level, concentrate and avoid distractions, be good to yourself. Treat your errors positively; record them either mentally or by writing them down and then forget them while playing the match at hand. Correct them when it is time to practice.

Remember to breathe deeply and slowly as well as slow your walking pace down as the tension level rises.

PSYCH-OUTS

Much has been written in recent years about how to psych out your opposition. You will be much better off to apply the positive approach utilized in this book and do every- thing possible to perform up to your own ability. Don't distract yourself from trying to win by destroying your oppo- nent. Simply recognize that reacting to any environmental situation on an emotional rather than on an intellectual level, will be detrimental to your game. When confronted with such situations, induce relaxation and respond in a rational manner.

GOLFING WITH A PARTNER

For the large number of country club golfers a major per- centage of your tournament experience will be in best-ball style tournaments. Without a doubt, psychological aspects of team play will be a major determinant of success or fail- ure.

Many golfers have carefully considered the strategy of selecting a partner. The two most typical questions are: (1) Should I play with a partner with similar skills and abili- ties?, or (2) Should I play with a partner with very different skills and abilities? These are very pertinent questions in order to insure that two people can communicate effectively and build, rather than destroy, confidence in each other. If two golfers cannot communicate, their chances for success are diminished greatly. Some teams seem to automatically communicate and develop into successful golfers. Many others however have all the prerequisite skills to be effective but never achieve success in team matches. For such teams, success will only come from improved communication.

COMMUNICATION

The relationship which you have with your partner is directly related to your ability to communicate openly and effectively. For example, there may be aspects of your golf game about which you feel uncomfortable. You must find a way to share these thoughts, fears, or confidences with your partner. On the other hand, your partner may observe some things about your game which you may not even realize. Try to realize that (1) there are things that you communicate openly; (2) there are elements which your partner observes, but which are blind to you; (3) there are things that you know, but that your partner does not realize; and

	Known to Self	Not Known to Self
Known to Others	Q1 Open	Q2 Blind
Not Known to Others	Hidden Q3	Unknown Q4

(4) there may be important characteristics of your golf game which are not obvious to either you or your partner.

In 1955 two experts in group dynamics, Luft and Ingham,* illustrated these relationships in terms of awareness with what has been called the Johari Window (see Fig., adapted from Luft & Ingham). The model can be very helpful to the golfing team, and can be viewed as having four separate quadrants. Quadrant 1 (Q1), the areas of free activity, or open area, refers to behavior and motivation known to you and your partner. In a new team, Q1 is very small; there is not much open or free and spontaneous interaction. As the team remains intact for extended periods of time, this openness grows larger, and in general both partners are more likely to be freer and perceive others as they really are. Quadrant 2, the blind area, is where others can see things in ourselves of which we are unaware. Sometimes our partners can see weaknesses in our game or motivation which are not recognized by us. Quadrant 2 will shrink slowly in size, particularly if we become aware of our strengths and weaknesses, and quit hiding them, either consciously or unconsciously. Quadrant 3, the avoided or hidden area, represents things we know but fail to reveal to others (often weaknesses or skills we feel sensitive about). These hidden strengths and weaknesses are reduced in size

* Luft, J. and Ingham, H. *The Johari Window, A Graphic Model of Interpersonal Awareness.* University of California, Los Angeles, Extension Office. Proceedings of the Western Training Laboratory in Group Development, August 1955.

and number as our communication becomes more open and Q1 expands. As an atmosphere of mutual trust is developed there is less need to hide pertinent thoughts or feelings. Quadrant 4, the area of unknown activity, points to the area where neither you nor your partner are aware of certain behaviors or motives. We can, however, assume these exist because with time, some of these things surface and become known to one or both of you. It is at this point in time that we realize these unknowns were influencing our play and relationships all along.

A basic goal is to increase the area of free open activity in Q1 and reduce the size of Quadrants 2, 3, and 4. The largest reduction will occur in Q3 as you become more open and sharing with your partner. The likelihood of much better and more positive use of the knowledge and skills of both partners will increase with greater openness. Team morale will also be positively influenced. Opinions and ideas will be communicated more often and less time will be spent on self-defensive and ego-involving behaviors which are likely to hinder your golf performance.

IMPROVING COMMUNICATION
WITH YOUR PARTNER

The stated results of improved communication no doubt appear to be quite positive. How then do we go about the process of change and where do we start?

In the early stages of team formation both partners will think and feel in an independent manner. In other words, each member will tend to rely on his or her own feelings, impressions, and judgements as a guide to behavior. There will always be times when independent action will be required but an important quality of the mature team is interdependence of members upon one another.

Golfers who wish to improve the communication in their best-ball team must be willing to open themselves up to their partner. Communication will not change if this doesn't happen. Communication is a two-way street. Both golfers must be willing to be flexible, open and honest.

The following is a listing of questions that best-ball partners can use to increase their cohesiveness and performance efficiency. Both partners must make a commitment to being as open and honest as possible if they truly wish to benefit to the fullest.

1. What are your greatest strengths as a golfer? What are your best shots? Are you a fast or slow starter? Do you recover from trouble well? Are you steady? Are you a great scrambler? Do you shoot a lot of birdies but also a lot of bogies? Do you play your best in clutch situations? Are you a spot putter?
2. What are your major weaknesses as a golfer? What are your poorest shots? If you start slowly, are you in trouble? Are you inconsistent? Are you a poor putter? Are you weak on putts breaking to the right?
3. When do you play with the most confidence? Do you need to hit first? Do you get better when playing with a lead?
4. When do you get the most anxious? Do you feel a lot of stress that hurts you when you hit first? Do you fall apart if your partner is OB and you must hit second? Do you usually have trouble on the closing holes?
5. Which behaviors by a partner tend to help you play better? Do you need to be positively encouraged? Do you need to feel that you are contributing to the team? Do you need to talk over strategy a lot? Do you prefer not to talk much? Do you like lining up your own putts, or would you prefer to have your partner help you?

BEYOND COMMUNICATION

Clearly, interdependence is important to team success. This does not mean however that you should give up personal responsibility for your team's success or failure. Recognize that you are at least one-half of the team and how you perform will be crucial.

Do not allow yourself to become the kind of partner who takes responsibility for the match outcome when you win, but blames failures on your partner. Making negative comments about your own play following a match will not hurt your team. But making negative statements about your partner's performance to other golfers can be retold to your partner and hinder your future success.

Try at all times to encourage and help your partner to play better. Listen to your partner when he or she speaks to you on the course. Show your interest and respect. Prevent at all times negative emotional behaviors from hindering your open communication.

Recognize when you can help your partner and when your helpful advice is of little value. The best way to assess this situation is to try and view the incident from your partner's perception rather than from your own. Often they differ markedly. If your partner is playing great, keep your comments positive, but general. For example, if your partner is driving particularly well, do not start saying, "Gee, you are really staying down on the ball and keeping your weight behind it." Such statements will only sensitize your partner to the details of the swing and force it to be a conscious effort rather than subconscious performance. Your comments should be kept general, such as, "You're really playing well today"; or "Your drives are super."

If your partner is playing poorly, do everything you can to take the pressure off and build confidence. Behave as though your partner's play is not bothering you. Do not try to become your partner's coach. He can probably work out of his problems faster without your constant advice (especially if you are in the middle of a critical match). The first time your partner makes a good swing or shot, use it as an opportunity to build confidence and get it going well again.

In essence, the answer to developing success in team matches is to know when to play your own game rather than becoming ego involved and playing someone else's. Know your partner and behave in a manner that will help him or her play up to his/her ability. Remember, it is probably more difficult to concentrate when playing with a partner than when you are playing alone. But success in team play can be a more rewarding experience for you and your partner than individual play. It will also require more awareness of your partner's needs than any other golfing competition that you have ever played in before.

10

Setting Your Goals and Attaining Them

The information presented so far can be of great value to you. It can also be of little or no value. As mentioned in Chapter 7, unless you were born an unbelievably gifted golfer you need to set goals. Plan the program effectively, and then have the self-discipline and desire to practice regularly. The following is a program that may be effective so you know you won't be wasting practice, and you will be motivated because you will be continually seeing your improvement.

There are at least six steps which are crucial to the goal setting process:

Step 1—Know Yourself
How good of a golfer am I now?
How good would I like to be?
Why, in the past, have I not progressed as I would like?
Am I self-disciplined?
Do I concentrate when I practice?
Am I willing to take responsibility for my achievement or would I rather blame others or bad luck for my success or failure?

Step 2—Skills Required for Golf
What are the skills required for success in golf?
Do I understand the golf swing, strategies and rules?
Do I understand the mental aspects of golf?
Do I know what muscle groups require strength for gaining distance?
Do I know which muscle groups must be relaxed to consistently hit the ball long and straight?
Do I have enough flexibility to develop a full turn?

Step 3—Self-Evaluation
What are my greatest strengths as a golfer?
What are my greatest weaknesses as a golfer?
Do I know how to go about improving each of them?
How much time am I willing to put into my practicing?
Do I tend to practice only the shots I enjoy?
Am I practicing perfectly to ensure success or am I just putting in time?
Do I tend to practice my strengths, or the shots I am already good at with very little time on my weaknesses?
Is the amount of time I spend on each shot related not only to what needs the most improvement but also the shots which mean the most to golf success?

Step 4—Define Your Goals
   Define your goals. Be sure that your goals are challenging but realistic. Be certain that if you put the time and effort planned into them that you will attain them. Once you attain them you will automatically raise your level of aspiration and raise your goals.

Step 5—Plan
Plan how you will meet your goals.
How much time do I have to attain my long-term goals?
How can I best use the resources at my disposal in the time I have to learn?
What will my plan of attack be for attaining each of my subgoals?
How much will I attain each day, week, month, year?

Step 6—Evaluate Your Progress
Evaluate your progress.
Are you progressing effectively?
Is my improvement on schedule?
If not, why not, and what changes am I going to make?
Do I have appropriate equipment available?
Do I have confidence in my instructor and my swing or is a change needed?
Make a decision and stick with it.

SAMPLE PROGRAM

Evaluate Where You Are at Present
   Distance. Go to the practice tee and hit twenty balls with each club while swinging smoothly, and determine your distance

for each club. Compare your distance to other golfers at the level that you are striving for. If you are not hitting the ball as far as you should, why not? Poor swing mechanics? Lack of leg and upper body strength? Lack of flexibility? Identify the problem, establish a remediation program based on your goals, and go to work.

Accuracy. Go back to the practice tee and set up targets with twenty-foot length and twenty-foot width boundaries at a distance described above. (May be wider for wood shots.) Hit twenty balls with each club and record how many of each lands within the boundaries. Identify your weakest clubs or shots. Start scheduling your practice. Be sure to go through this process with putting, chipping, sand shots, etc.

Plan for Attaining Your Goals

   Goal—Get handicap from thirteen to ten

   Major Weakness—Inaccurate driver. Distance is acceptable.

   Date—March 1, 1981

   Present Skill Level—Can hit target forty feet by forty feet, 110
       yards away—an average of three out of twenty attempts.
       Tested on three consecutive days. (Record on appropriate
       date on calendar.)

   Long-Term Goal—To hit target area an average of twelve times
       out of twenty attempts. (Record on calendar for June 1.)

Assess Reasons for Inaccuracy

   Set time schedule for shot and long-term goals

   Long-Term Goals—Accomplish by June 1

   Improvement Required—Nine shots better out of twenty at-
       tempted

   Total Practice Days—Ninety

   Time Per Day Spent Practicing No. One Wood at Present—
       Eight to ten practice shots per day

   Time Per Day Planned Next Ninety Days—Minimum of
       twenty-five driver shots per day hitting each shot as though
       on course, going through complete shot routine and simulat-
       ing OB to left or right. (Record on calendar under Planned.)

   Short-Term Goal—Eight out of twenty by April 1. (Record
       on calendar for April 1.) You will be likely to experience
       rapid improvement at the lower skill level. As you get better,
       it will slow down because there is less room for improvement
       as your skill level gets higher. Record each day you practice
       the number of balls hit. Every two weeks record your accu-

racy score on test on three consecutive days. Record your test score. If you are progressing ahead of time, raise your goals. If progressing too slowly, check to see if you are practicing correctly. Are you establishing a target? Do you need to devote more time to practice with the one wood?

Continue to practice on schedule. Each day record your amount of practice on this weakness on your calendar. Retest every two weeks and mark your score on the calendar. This serves as both a daily reminder that you are working on a goal and a motivator by charting your improvement. Keep it on your desk.

Spend ten to fifteen minutes each day inducing relaxation, making a self-statement to your commitment to improving, visually imagining going from preshot routine to

finish of hitting your driver, finishing with internal rehearsal. This is very important. Do not fail to allow yourself
time for your mental training.

DEVELOPING A POSITIVE MENTAL SET

Spend ten to fifteen minutes each day inducing relaxation
and utilizing imagery. An ideal time is just prior to going
to sleep at night (unless you tend to go to sleep before
getting into your imagery). Once you are relaxed, use external imagery to go through hitting your driver from preliminary routine, to set-up, to post-shot routine. Next, practice
internal imagery of hitting your driver from preliminary
routine, to set-up, to post-shot routine to develop feel. Finally, and very importantly, visually imagine yourself going
through tomorrow's planned practice session and recording
your results on your calendar. Think positively about how
good you will feel when you play well in June as a result
of your efforts. If any self-doubts enter your mind, tell yourself to STOP and utilize self-talk in a positive manner. Talk
to yourself about the improvements that will result from
perfect practice and planning for success.

11
Onward and Downward

You are now ready to embark upon a most enjoyable and self-satisfying task. You now have a strategy that will help you to find out just how good a golfer you can become. Get into it and enjoy the process. It is the enjoyment of this process, this search for your limits, that can be so very exciting. Soon you will be playing golf better than you ever have in your life.

Be sure that as you begin your new approach to golf you continuously encourage yourself. If others try to discourage you from believing in yourself, don't listen. Be your own motivator. Make yourself a successful golfer.

Sometimes success-motivated golfers focus only on the negative aspects of their golf game. As we have mentioned earlier in this book, you must work to eliminate your weaknesses. But don't become so obsessed with your weaknesses and the negative qualities in your mental approach to golf that you never praise or practice your strengths and positive qualities. Be good to yourself. Go ahead and be modest and humble when you talk to others, but when you talk to yourself, be confident and praise yourself. Listen to the statements made by the pros; but when they make statements, realize that what they say in public may not be what they say to themselves when it is time to play. You can be sure that despite their praise for others, they believe in themselves.

When it is time to perform, dwell on your strengths and feel good about yourself. Look for something good about every shot that you hit. Don't let yourself slip into the bad

habit of criticizing yourself after every shot, or imagining the worst before you even hit the ball.

As you get ready to put the ideas in this book into practice, decide that you will stick with them for an extended time period. Believe that if you do, you will improve. Do not question your commitment. Give yourself a chance to be successful.

Every night as you go to bed, close your eyes and relax. Reassure yourself that you are on your way to success. You will control your mind and your body under the stress of competition. If you make a mistake you will understand why and be able to self-correct so that it won't happen again.

Let your mind wander off to the golf course. See and feel yourself playing great golf. Hit every shot perfectly and enjoy it. Feel good. Start off on the first hole. Hit a great tee shot. Your position is perfect. Lay your second shot up close to the pin. Sink the putt and go to the next hole. Your swing feels smooth and easy. You are lost in the game of golf. Continue to feel great for the entire round.

You are no longer afraid of challenges. You enjoy them. When faced with a hole bordered by out-of-bounds on both sides, accept the challenge and hit the perfect shot. Your swing is smooth. You feel good before you stroke your putts. You don't make them all, but you know that you have done your best. You are in control of your mind. You have put in your practice time and are ready to play because you are prepared, both physically and psychologically.

Golf is fun. You are getting better and better. Your efforts are paying off, and your scores are going down. Your confidence is going up, and you are swinging smoothly. You are hitting the ball consistently well. Your putting stroke feels great. Your clubs feel great in your hands.

HOLD IT.

You're there. You're

MASTERING YOUR MIND FOR WIN-NING GOLF!

Appendix

GOLF PERFORMANCE OBSERVATION
FORMS

The following observation forms are provided for your convenience so that you may tear them out and utilize them at any golf course.

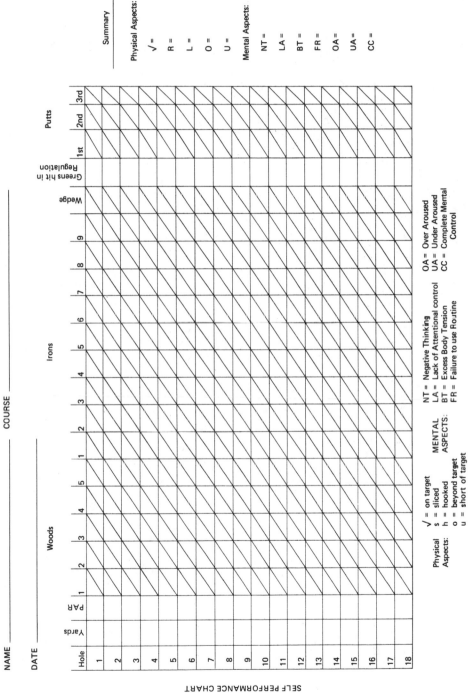

NAME _____   COURSE _____

DATE _____

SELF PERFORMANCE CHART

Hole	Yards	PAR	Woods					Irons									Wedge	Greens hit in Regulation	Putts		
			1	2	3	4	5	1	2	3	4	5	6	7	8	9			1st	2nd	3rd
1																					
2																					
3																					
4																					
5																					
6																					
7																					
8																					
9																					
10																					
11																					
12																					
13																					
14																					
15																					
16																					
17																					
18																					

Physical Aspects:
√ = on target
s = sliced
h = hooked
o = beyond target
u = short of target

MENTAL ASPECTS:
NT = Negative Thinking
LA = Lack of Attentional control
BT = Excess Body Tension
FR = Failure to use Routine
OA = Over Aroused
UA = Under Aroused
CC = Complete Mental Control

Summary

Physical Aspects:
√ =
R =
L =
O =
U =

Mental Aspects:
NT =
LA =
BT =
FR =
OA =
UA =
CC =

139

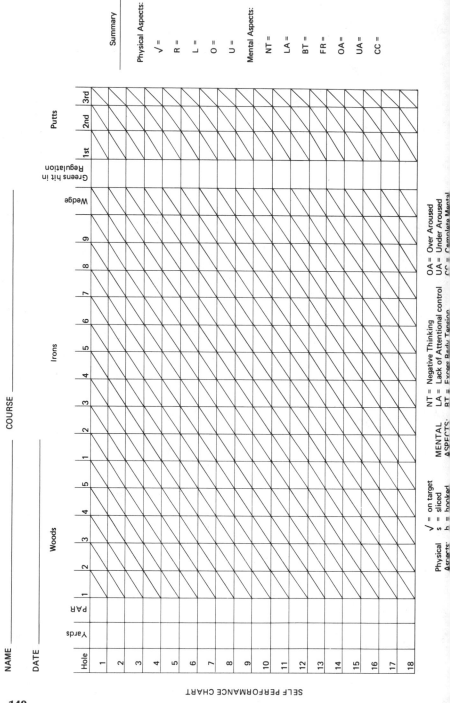

NAME _____

DATE _____

COURSE _____

140

SELF PERFORMANCE CHART

Hole	Yards	PAR	Woods 1	2	3	4	5	Irons 1	2	3	4	5	6	7	8	9	Wedge	Greens hit in Regulation	Putts 1st	2nd	3rd
1																					
2																					
3																					
4																					
5																					
6																					
7																					
8																					
9																					
10																					
11																					
12																					
13																					
14																					
15																					
16																					
17																					
18																					

Summary

Physical Aspects:

√ =

R =

L =

O =

U =

Mental Aspects:

NT =

LA =

BT =

FR =

OA =

UA =

CC =

Physical Aspects:
√ = on target
s = sliced
h = hooked

MENTAL ASPECTS:
NT = Negative Thinking
LA = Lack of Attentional control
BT = Excess Body Tension

OA = Over Aroused
UA = Under Aroused
CC = Complete Mental

NAME —————————— COURSE ——————————
DATE ——————————

SELF PERFORMANCE CHART

Hole	Yards	PAR	Woods 1 2 3 4 5	Irons 1 2 3 4 5 6 7 8 9	Wedge	Greens hit in Regulation	Putts 1st 2nd 3rd
1							
2							
3							
4							
5							
6							
7							
8							
9							
10							
11							
12							
13							
14							
15							
16							
17							
18							

Physical Aspects:
√ = on target
s = sliced
h = hooked
o = beyond target
u = short of target

MENTAL ASPECTS:
NT = Negative Thinking
LA = Lack of Attentional control
BT = Excess Body Tension
FR = Failure to use Routine
OA = Over Aroused
UA = Under Aroused
CC = Complete Mental Control

Summary

Physical Aspects:
√ =
R =
L =
O =
U =

Mental Aspects:
NT =
LA =
BT =
FR =
OA =
UA =
CC =

141

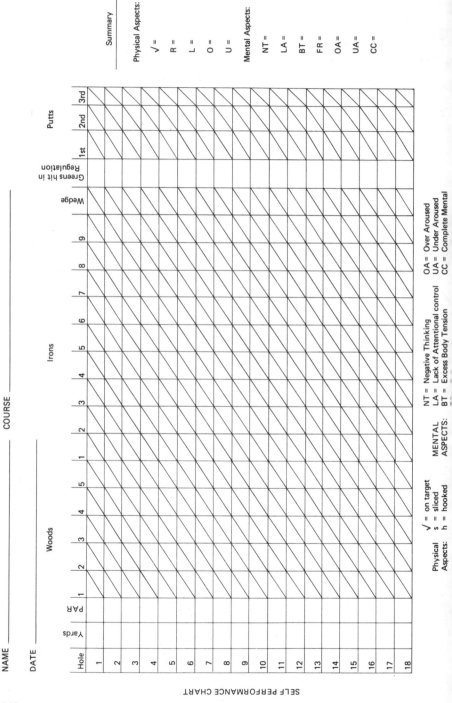

NAME _____ COURSE _____

DATE _____

Summary

Physical Aspects:

√ =
R =
L =
O =
U =

Mental Aspects:

NT =
LA =
BT =
FR =
OA =
UA =
CC =

Hole	Yards	PAR	Woods 1	2	3	4	5	Irons 1	2	3	4	5	6	7	8	9	Wedge	Greens hit in Regulation	Putts 1st	2nd	3rd
1																					
2																					
3																					
4																					
5																					
6																					
7																					
8																					
9																					
10																					
11																					
12																					
13																					
14																					
15																					
16																					
17																					
18																					

Physical Aspects: √ = on target   s = sliced   h = hooked

MENTAL ASPECTS:
NT = Negative Thinking
LA = Lack of Attentional control
BT = Excess Body Tension
OA = Over Aroused
UA = Under Aroused
CC = Complete Mental

SELF PERFORMANCE CHART

142

Index

Achievement plan, 16–17
  Caldwell, Rex, example of, 16–17
  and slumps, effect of on swing, 16
Anxiety, level of, and self-aware-ness, 71–72
Anxiety, physical effects of, 77–80
  controllability, 79
  decreased blood flow, 78
  fatigue, 79–80
  feel and coordination, lack of, 78
  and muscle tension, 78
  Palmer, Arnold, example of, 78–79
  past experience, 79
Anxiety, self-test for, 54–56
  scoring, 56
Attention, control of, 48–51
  main areas, 49
  width and direction, 50–51
Attention, depth of, 40–41
Attention-distraction self-evalua-tion inventory, 45–47
  and narrow focus, 47
Attention, factors of in golf, 41–43
  focus switching, 41–42
  and narrow focus, 42
  practice vs. perfection, 42–43
  sequence of, 43
Attention style, recognition of, 43–44
  and analysis, 44
  excess width, 44

Attention style (continued)
  and feelings, involvement with, 43–44
Attention, width, 40–41

Body, control of by mind, 31–33
  actual and imagined experi-ences, mental identity of, 32
  physical reactions, 32
  Snead, Sam, experience of, 32
  and subjective truth, 32
Breath control, 86–88
  in golf, 87
  in other fields, 86

Coaching, of self, 118–19
Commitment to improvement, 14
Communication, 120–25
  points to remember, 120–21, 123–25
  activity quadrants, 121–22
  Johari windows, 121
Concentration, improvement tech-niques, 49–50
  and distractions, 50
  and others, 50
  and word TARGET, 49
Concentration, and self-discipline, 97–98
  discussion, 97
  and mind games, 97–98
Confidence, building of, 25–26
  champions, 25, 26
  and self-concept, 26